Existence, space and architecture

Christian Norberg-Schulz

Existence, Space & Architecture

PRAEGER PUBLISHERS
New York · Washington

Series Editor: Mary Kling

BOOKS THAT MATTER
Published in the United States of America in 1971
by Praeger Publishers, Inc.
111 Fourth Avenue, New York, N.Y. 10003

© 1971 in Oslo, Norway, by Christian Norberg-Schulz
All rights reserved
First published in Great Britain in 1971 by Studio Vista Limited
Blue Star House, Highgate Hill, London N19
Library of Congress Catalog Card Number: 70-128598
Printed in Great Britain

Contents

A child 'concretizes' its
existential space

Foreword

The problem of architectural theory may be approached in many different ways. In *Intentions in Architecture* (1963) I tried to indicate the various factors which determine the architectural totality, as well as their logical interrelations. A semeiological approach is at present followed by many scholars, based on French structuralism and the linguistic theories of Noam Chomsky. The development of a coherent method of analysing the building task has also been attempted, notably by Christopher Alexander, while others, such as Robert Venturi, aim at a renewal of the theory of architectural form.

In the present book we offer a new approach to the problem of architectural space. So far, the discussion of architectural space has been dominated by naïve realism, either disguised as studies in 'architectural perception' or as tri-dimensional geometry. In both cases the basic problem of space as a dimension of human existence is omitted with the result that the space concept is nowadays often regarded as outdated or even superfluous. I still believe, however, that the space concept is particularly suited for the analysis of the human environment. On the basis of a theory of 'existential space', I therefore develop the idea that architectural space may be understood as a concretization of environmental schemata or images, which form a necessary part of man's general orientation or 'being in the world'. I believe thereby to have established a simple and useful key to the architectural totality. The book is indebted to philosophical, psychological and architectural studies, to which reference is given in the text. In particular I would like to thank all those with whom I have had the opportunity to discuss my ideas: Arne Korsmo (Trondheim)†, Sigfried Giedion (Zürich)†, Kjell Lund (Oslo), Colin St John Wilson (Cambridge), George Baird (Toronto), Charles Jencks (London), Joseph Rykwert (London), Hans Sedlmayr (Salzburg), Ferdinand Schuster (Graz), Carlo Cassola (Grosseto), and last but not least, Paolo Portoghesi (Rome) to whom this book is dedicated.

CNS

Any functional action
has particular spatial
implications

1 The concept of space

'Like the spider with its web, so every subject weaves relationships between itself and particular properties of objects; the many strands are then woven together and finally form the basis of the subject's very existence.'

Jakob von Uexküll

The system of spaces

Man's interest in space has existential roots. It stems from a need to grasp vital relations in his environment, to bring meaning and order into a world of events and actions. Basically, man orients to 'objects', that is, he adapts physiologically and technologically to physical things, he interacts with other people, and he grasps the abstract realities, or 'meanings', which are transmitted through the various languages created for the purpose of communication. His orientation to the different objects may be cognitive as well as affective, but in either case it aims at the establishment of a dynamic equilibrium between him and his environment. Talcott Parsons says: 'Action consists of the structures and processes by which human beings form meaningful intentions and, more or less successfully, implement them in concrete situations.'[1] Most of man's actions comprise a *spatial* aspect, in the sense that the objects of orientation are distributed according to such relations as inside and outside; far away and close by; separate and united; and continuous and discontinuous. Space, therefore, is not a particular category of orientation, but an aspect of any orientation. It should, however, be stressed that it is only *one* aspect of the total orientation. To be able to carry out his intentions, man has to 'understand' spatial relations and unify them in a 'space concept'.

While the *pragmatic space* of animals is a function of inborn instincts, man has to *learn* what orientation he needs in order to act. In the languages of early or primitive civilizations, therefore, we find terms which express and communicate spatial relations, such as above and below, before and behind, right and left. The terms, however, are not abstract, but have direct reference to man himself as well as to his environment and express his 'position' in the world. Certain African languages, for instance, use the same word for 'eye' and 'in front of'.[2] The space of the ancient Egyptians was determined by the particular geography of the country, and their language introduced the directions 'downstream' and 'upstream' rather than north and south. In both cases it is clear that a *cognitive concept* of space had not been abstracted from the direct experience of spatial relations. The spatial intuitions of the primitive are concrete orientations which refer to objects and localities and therefore have a strong emotional colour.

The Greek philosophers, however, made space an object of reflection. Parmenides represented a transitory position when he maintained that space as such cannot be imagined and therefore is non-existent, but Leucippos considered space a reality, though it has no bodily existence. Plato took the problem further in *Timaeus*, introducing geometry as the science of space, but it was

1 T. Parsons *Societies* 1966, p. 5

2 H. Werner *Einführung in die Entwicklungspsychologie* 1953, p. 120

3 Titus Lucretius Carus *De Rerum Natura* I, 420

4 I. Kant, 'Von dem ersten Grunde des Unterschiedes der Gegenden in Raume' *Gesammelte Werke* (Akademie-Ausgabe), II, p. 376

5 A. Einstein *Geometrie und Erfahrung* 1921, p. 3

6 H. Reichenbach *The Rise of Scientific Philosophy* 1951.

7 For a more complete discussion of perception see C. Norberg-Schulz *Intentions in Architecture* 1963, pp. 27ff

8 J. Piaget *The Psychology of Intelligence* 1950.

left to Aristotle to develop a theory of 'place' (topos). For him space was the sum of all places, a dynamic field with directions and qualitative properties. His approach may be considered as an attempt to systematize primitive, pragmatic space, but it also fore-shadows certain present-day concepts. Later theories of space were based on Euclidean geometry rather than Aristotle and defined space as infinite and homogeneous – one of the basic dimensions of the world. Thus Lucretius says: 'All nature is based on two things; there are bodies, and there is emptiness in which these bodies have their place, and in which they move'.[3] 1800 years later Kant still regarded space as a basic *a priori* category of human understanding, different from and independent of matter.[4] A particularly important elaboration of the theory of Euclidean space occurred in the seventeenth century with the introduction of the orthogonal co-ordinate system (Descartes).

The idea that Euclidean geometry gives a faithful representation of physical space collapsed with the creation of non-Euclidean geometries in the nineteenth century and with the theory of relativity. It was demonstrated that such geometries give a clearer approximation of physical space, and still more important, it was recognized that any geometry is a human construct rather than something found in nature. Thus Einstein says:

'When mathematical propositions refer to reality they are not certain; when they are certain, they do not refer to reality.'[5]

The ancient concept of a unified space, therefore, was split in several 'spaces': concrete physical spaces (micro, everyday and macro), and abstract mathematical spaces invented by man to describe the former with a greater or lesser degree of approximation.[6] The theory of relativity carried us even further, substituting the former idea of lumps of matter in a three-dimensional space, with a series of events in a four-dimensional space-time.

The physical and mathematical space concepts, however, satisfy only a small part of man's original need for orientation. By quantifying the primitive total experience a *cognitive* world of abstract relations resulted, which has little direct reference to everyday life. Although man conserved fragments of the original intuitions, certain aspects of his existence thereby became impoverished, such as the emotional relationship to the environment. We therefore ought to supplement the space concepts mentioned above, with others covering the *affective* aspects of behaviour.

The problem of 'human' space has been studied by psychologists for about a hundred years. Taking up the question of man's experience of his environment, it has been proved that *space perception* is a complex process, where many variables are involved. We do not simply perceive a world which is common to all of us, as naïve realists maintain, but different worlds which are a product of our motivations and past experiences.[7] In general, perception aims at valid assumptions about the nature of the environment, and these assumptions vary according to the situations in which we are taking part. A car-driver bases his actions on different assumptions from those of a pedestrian in the same street. Perception mediates a world which could also very well be described as 'events in a four-dimensional space-time'.

Just as physics aims at a structural description of physical events by means of mathematical models, psychology ought to describe the structure of psychic processes by means of a system of abstract concepts. Like those used in physics, early psychological concepts had a static, absolute character, but recently a more dynamic approach has been introduced. The absolute 'laws' of Gestalt psychology, for instance, have been replaced by Piaget's more flexible 'schemata'. A schema may be defined as a typical reaction to a situation. They are formed during mental development through the interaction between the individual and his environment and by this process a man's actions or 'operations' are grouped into coherent wholes.[8] Piaget describes the process as a combination of 'assimilation' and 'accommodation', 'assimilation' referring to the action of the organism on surrounding objects, and 'accommodation' to the opposite state. Thus the organism, rather than submitting passively to the environment, modifies it by imposing on it a certain structure of its own. 'Mental assimilation is thus the incorporation of objects into patterns of behaviour.'[9] Piaget ends by defining 'adaptation' as 'an equilibrium between assimilation and accommodation'.[10]

It is highly necessary that the organism should acquire schemata which directly mediate a three-dimensional world. Piaget shows that our 'space consciousness' is based upon operational schemata, that is, experiences with things. The space schemata may be of very different kinds, and the individual normally possesses more than one schema, to allow him a satisfactory perception of diverse situations. The schemata are culturally determined and comprise qualitative properties resulting from the need for affective orientation to the environment. Piaget sums up his investigations with these words: 'It is quite obvious that the perception of space involves a gradual construction and certainly does not exist ready-made at the outset of mental development.'[11]

We thus see that the synthetic space of primitive man has been split into several specialized constructs which serve us in our orientation and adaptation to different aspects of the environment. In addition to the cognitive spaces, we have within the psychological dimension to distinguish between immediate *perceptual space* and the more stable *space schemata*. The latter are composed of elements which have a certain invariance, such as universal elementary structures (archetypes) and socially or culturally conditioned structures, and, of course, some personal idiosyncrasies. Together these make up man's 'image' of his environment, that is, a stable system of three-dimensional relations between meaningful objects. We will therefore unify the schemata in the concept *existential space*. Perceptual space, on the contrary, is egocentric and varies continuously, although the variations are linked to form meaningful totalities (experiences) because they are assimilated to the subjects' schemata, which are in turn somewhat modified by the new experience. We have so far distinguished between five

space concepts: the pragmatic space of physical action, the perceptual space of immediate orientation, the existential space which forms man's stable image of his environment, the cognitive space of the physical world and the abstract space of pure logical relations. Pragmatic space integrates man with his natural, 'organic' environment, perceptual space is essential to his identity as a person, existential space makes him belong to a social and cultural totality,[12] cognitive space means that he is able to think about space, and logical space, finally, offers the tool to describe the others. The series shows a growing abstraction from pragmatic space at the 'lowest' level to logical space at the top, that is, a growing content of 'information'. Cybernetically, thus, the series is controlled from the top, while its vital energy rises up from the bottom.[13]

One basic aspect, however, has still been omitted. From remote times man has not only acted in space, perceived space, existed in space and thought about space, but he has also created space to express the structure of his world as a real *imago mundi*. We may call this creation *expressive* or *artistic space*, and it finds its place in the hierarchy next to the top, together with cognitive space. Like cognitive space, expressive space needs a more abstract construct for its description, a space concept which systematizes the possible properties of expressive spaces. We may call this 'aesthetic space'. The creation of expressive space has always been the task of specialized persons, that is, builders, architects and planners, while aesthetic space has been studied by architectural theorists and philosophers. In the present book, therefore, we will talk about *architectural space* rather than expressive space, and aesthetic space as the theory of architectural space. In a certain sense, any man who chooses a place in his environment to settle and live, is a creator of expressive space. He makes his environment meaningful by assimilating it to his purposes at the same time as he accommodates to the conditions it offers.

What then are the relations between architectural space and the other members of the system? Architectural space certainly has to adapt itself to the needs of organic action as

9 J. Piaget *The Psychology of Intelligence* 1950, p. 8

10 J. Piaget *The Psychology of Intelligence* 1950, p. 8

11 J. Piaget and B. Inhelder *The Child's Conception of Space* 1956, p. 6

12 The social basis of schemata is discussed by Piaget in *The Psychology of Intelligence* p. 156ff., where he stresses that the social environment in part determines the interactions from which the schemata stem. He says: 'Without interchange of thought and co-operation with others the individual would never come to group his operations into a coherent whole: in this sense, therefore, operational grouping presupposes social life' (p. 163), and further: 'The grouping consists essentially in a freeing of the individuals perceptions and spontaneous intuitions from the egocentric viewpoint . . .' (p. 164)

13 The proposed model is related to Talcott Parsons' 'System of Action' (*Societies* p. 28). His system is divided into four sub-systems which form 'environments' to each other: the behavioural organism, the personality system, the social system and the cultural system

14 For a discussion of the concept of 'concretization' see C. Norberg-Schulz *Intentions in Architecture* 1963, pp. 61ff

well as facilitating orientation through perception. It could also 'illustrate' certain cognitive theories of space, as when building a Cartesian co-ordinate system with concrete materials. But above all it is related to the space schemata of man's individual and public world. Obviously man's schemata are created through interaction with existing architectural spaces, and when these do not satisfy him, that is, when his image becomes confused or too unstable, he will have to change architectural space. Architectural space, therefore, can be defined as a concretization of man's existential space.[14]

The concept of space in architectural theory

15 B. Zevi *Architecture and Space* 1957. His space concept seems to be a combination of action space and Euclidean space, as he says: 'Architecture is like a large hollow structure into which man enters and around which he moves'. (author's own trans)

16 P. Frankl *Die Entwicklungsphasen der neueren Baukunst* 1914; A. E. Brinckmann *Baukunst* 1956; P. Zucker *Town and Square* 1959

17 S. Giedion *Space, Time and Architecture* 1941

18 S. Giedion *The Eternal Present: The Beginnings of Architecture* 1964

19 S. Giedion *The Eternal Present: The Beginnings of Architecture* 1964, pp. 522ff

20 S. Giedion 'Die Ungreifbarkeit des Raumes' *Neue Zürcher Zeitung* 22/8-1965

Much attention has been given to the problem of space in architecture. We do not need to discuss the spatial implications of early theories here; rather we should concentrate on the actual use of the term. Recently, as a matter of fact, 'space' has become a catchword, which to many critics seems to explain without further qualifications what architecture is all about. Bruno Zevi, thus, defines architecture as the 'art of space', but he does not really define the nature of the space he talks about.[15] Obviously his concept of space is naïvely realistic, as is the case with most writers on the subject, to whom space is a uniformly extended 'material' which can be 'modelled' in various ways. Many important investigations, however, *have* been made on this basis; I may for instance refer to the works of Paul Frankl, A. E. Brinckmann and Paul Zucker.[16] After all, the question of how to articulate Euclidean space is one aspect of the more comprehensive problem of architectural space.

Sigfried Giedion is probably the writer who has contributed most to the actualization of the space concept. In his book *Space, Time and Architecture*[17] he put the problem of space at the centre of the development of modern architecture, and in later works he has presented the history of architecture as a succession of 'space conceptions'.[18] In general he distinguishes between three basic conceptions. 'The first architectural space conception was concerned with the emanating power of volumes, their relations with one another, and their interaction. This binds the Egyptian and Greek developments together. Both proceed outward from the volume.

The dome of Hadrian's Pantheon at the beginning of the second century signalized the complete breakthrough of the second space conception. From that time on, the concept of architectural space was almost indistinguishable from the concept of hollowed-out interior space.'[19] The third space conception, which is still in its infancy, is chiefly concerned with the problem of the interaction between inner and outer space. Giedion thus leaves the idea of a mechanistic combination of units in Euclidean space behind, and attempts to describe the qualitative differences which are related to the general development of man's image of the world. Thus he says:

'The process by which a spatial image can be transposed into the emotional sphere is expressed by the spatial concept. It yields information on the relation between man and his environment. It is the spiritual expression of the reality that confronts him. The world that lies before him is changed by it. It forces him to project graphically his own position if he wants to come to terms with it.'[20]

Giedion here approaches the concept of existential space, but he does not make his idea philosophically precise. His approach is still too naïvely realistic, although he makes some references to the process of visual perception.

Most studies of architectural space still suffer from a lack of conceptual definition. In general they can be divided into two classes: those which are based on Euclidean space and study its 'grammar', and those which try to develop a theory of space on the basis of perception psychology. The Euclidean approach has recently been stimulated by the importance of three-dimensional geometry in connection with space-frames, prefabricated building systems and certain utopian city-planning schemes.[21] A typical attempt at systematization is represented by Walter Netsch's 'Field Theory'.[22] Netsch and many others believe they have found the key to the organization of architectural space in a systematic development of two- and three-dimensional patterns of geometrical character. It cannot be denied that geometry forms a part of the syntactics of architectural space, but, as I will try and show later, it has to be integrated in a more comprehensive theory to become meaningful. So far we can only point out that man's image of the environment, his existential space, obviously cannot be described solely in terms of geometrical grids. Christopher Alexander also centres his attention upon the concept of pattern, but defines it in terms of function rather than geometry, and thereby takes an important step towards the development of a useful theory of architectural space.[23]

The cool and abstract character of combinational geometry has led many writers to maintain that architectural space is basically 'different' from mathematical space. The criticism of a purely quantitative study of space was already voiced by the art historian Hans Jantzen in 1938, who wrote:

'Formalistic spatial analysis that examines the space represented in the work of art as a separable stylistic form must be complemented by a consideration of the represented space as a dimension of the meaning embodied within the work of art.'[24]

The Swiss critic Vogt-Göknil takes this criticism as her point of departure, and tries to develop a theory of architectural space as 'Umraum' (surrounding space). She does not, however, recognize the fundamental difference between perceptual and existential space, and therefore gets stuck with imprecise terms like 'Erlebnis eines Raumes' (perceived space) and 'Gesamteindruck' (total impression) or talks about 'an un-biassed encounter with the spatial totality'.[25] As a matter of fact, the word 'Umraumerlebnis' (perception of surrounding space), which appears in the title of her book, ought to be defined in terms of perception psychology. To illustrate her thesis, Vogt-Göknil discusses three types of space: 'Der weite Raum' (extensive space), 'der enge Raum' (limited space), 'der gerichtete Raum' (ordered space). In doing this, she touches upon several important properties of existential space, but lacking a coherent system of well-defined concepts, her research could not arrive at any useful general conclusions.

Vogt-Göknil's attempt to replace the current quantitative space concept with a more 'human' concept based on man's 'experience of space', is characteristic of numerous recent essays on the subject. Günther Nitschke, thus, in his article 'Anatomie der gelebten Umwelt' contrasts Euclidean space with 'experienced or concrete space', which he defines as follows:

'It has a centre which is perceiving man,
and it therefore has an excellent
system of directions which changes with
the movements of the human body; it is
limited and in no sense neutral, in other
words it is finite, heterogeneous,
subjectively defined and perceived;
distances and directions are fixed relative
to man . . .'[26]

Nitschke here gives a good definition of perceptual space, but he does not recognize the fact that any perception must be referred to a more stable system of schemata (images) to become meaningful. It is impossible to discuss architectural space systematically when perceptual space is taken as the point of departure. What one describes in this way are subjective architectural *experiences*, and one would have to arrive at the absurd conclusion that 'architecture comes into being only when experienced'. It is, therefore, nonsense to say that man is always the centre of *architectural* space, and that the directions of architectural space change with the movements of the human body. Architectural space certainly exists independently of the casual perceiver, and has centres and directions of its own.

21 See the works of A. Neumann, E. Schultze-Fielitz, the Archigram group, etc.

22 See W. Netsch 'Forms as Process' *Progressive Architecture* March 1969

23 C. Alexander *Notes on the Synthesis of Form* 1964

24 H. Jantzen 'Ueber den kunstgeschichtlichen Raumbegriff' *Sitzungsberichte der Bayerischen Akademie der Wissenschaften* 1938, p. 5

25 U. Vogt-Göknil *Architektonische Grundbegriffe und Umraumerlebnis* 1951

26 G. Nitschke 'Anatomie der gelebten Umwelt' *Bauen + Wohnen*, September 1968

27 J. Joedicke
'Vorbemerkungen zu einer
Theorie des
architektonischen Raumes,
zugleich Versuch einer
Standortbestimmung der
Architektur' *Bauen +
Wohnen*, September 1968

28 M. Leonard
'Humanizing Space'
Progressive Architecture,
April 1969

The same imprecise use of space concepts characterize Jürgen Joedicke's essay 'Vorbemerkungen zu einer Theorie des architektonischen Raumes'.[27] Joedicke stresses the importance of defining the spatial concept employed, and excludes mathematical space, economical space, geographical space, political space, as well as 'the space concept of O. F. Bollnow' (to which we shall return later). What he wants to talk about is 'space in architecture', starting from 'the axiom that buildings consist of spaces, and that architectural space therefore exists'(!). Joedicke, thus, starts with the well known approach of naïve realism, but later he says: 'We can speak of architectural space as an experiential space', and 'architectural space is tied to man and his perception'. His conclusion is logical: 'Space is the sum of successive perceptions of places'. What has been said above concerning the shortcomings of perceptual space as a point of departure for defining architectural space, also applies to the study of Joedicke.

An article by Michael Leonard with the characteristic title 'Humanizing Space',[28] contains many relevant observations and contributions towards a theory of space, but again the interpretation is hampered by the belief that the 'psychological dimensions of space' are found in immediate perception. Leonard says: ' . . . it is man who creates and experiences the *sensation* of space', and 'the final product in the perceptual process is a single sensation – a "feeling" about that particular place . . .'.

We may thus conclude that recent studies on the concept of space in relation to architecture have either tended to leave man out by discussing abstract geometry, or have made man 'enter' by reducing space and architecture to impressions, sensations and studies of 'effects'. In both cases space as an existential dimension, as a relation between man and his environment, has been forgotten. No wonder that many people are getting tired of the problem of space in architecture and want to talk about 'structure', 'system' or 'environment'. But little is gained by this attitude. Structures and environments concern the architect above all because of their spatial aspects, and sooner or later the problem of space has to be faced. In the following, therefore, we will discuss some contributions towards a more satisfactory theory of architectural space, a theory where space is really understood as a dimension of human existence, rather than as a dimension of thought or perception.

Architectural and existential space

A few years after the second world war, art historian Dagobert Frey and architect Rudolf Schwarz independently of each other formulated ideas which opened up new and inspiring possibilities. Let us start by taking a look at the little known contribution of Frey. In *Grundlegung zu einer vergleichenden Kunstwissenschaft* he introduces the concepts of 'path' (*Weg*) and 'goal' (*Mal*) to describe spatial structures. These concepts have the advantage of referring both to properties of existential space and concrete architectural space, and represent a true attempt at bridging intellectually the gap between man and his environment. Frey talks about 'archetypal motifs of world experience' and says:

'The goal already contains the path as its point of reference, directional indicator and ultimate end; and movement may be directed towards the goal, may emanate from it or may encircle it. All architecture is a structuring of space by means of a goal or path. Every house is an architecturally structured "path": the specific possibilities of movement and the drives towards movement as one proceeds from the entrance through the sequence of spatial entities have been pre-determined by the architectural structuring of that space and one experiences the space accordingly. But at the same time, in its relation to the surrounding space, it is a "goal", and we either advance towards this goal or depart from it.'[29]

Frey uses the word 'experience' (perception), but he implies that architectural space is not a function of this experience, rather it has a structure which ought to be experienced, because it expresses basic properties of human existence. We recognize here an early attempt at overcoming the abstract use of Euclidean space, as well as the limitations of immediate perceptual space.[30]

Related ideas were brought forward by Rudolf Schwarz in his magnificent but somewhat esoteric books *The Church Incarnate* and *Von der Bebauung der Erde*.[31] His carefully worked out concepts will be discussed in more detail later, but it should already be pointed out that his aim is to describe the fundamental structure of existence, of 'being in the world', and to translate this structure into concrete properties of architectural space. A few quotations may illustrate this point.

'Man cannot plan the world without designing himself.' 'At the time he took his land, he already decided the plan of his life and he measured the earth accordingly and placed the ground-plan of his historical existence within it.'

While Frey wanted to arrive at a better knowledge of history, and Schwarz aimed at a fuller understanding of existence as a basis for building and planning after the destructions of the war, the American Kevin Lynch takes the concrete problems of our modern cities as his point of departure. Lynch maintains that man's orientation presupposes an 'environmental image, a generalized mental picture of the exterior physical world . . . This image is the product both of immediate sensation and of the memory of past experience, and it is used to interpret information and to guide action . . . A good environmental image gives its possessor an important sense of emotional security.'[32] Lynch's concept of 'image' thus corresponds to the space schemata referred to above, and he tries to interpret the environment (city) in relation to an existential space. Lynch goes on to single out what he considers the fundamental properties of space, arriving at conclusions similar to those of Frey and Schwarz. Thus he says: 'The world may be organized around a set of focal points, or be broken into named regions, or be linked by remembered routes'.[33] As the works of Frey and Schwarz have remained known only to a relatively restricted number of people, Lynch's work which is more easily understood and actual has been met with great interest among architects and planners since it was published in 1960. Indeed it represents a very promising point of departure for further research on the problems of existential and architectural space, but so far little has been done. It may be that the general implications of Lynch's ideas have hardly been understood; rather than recognizing the true humanism of his work, he is often considered a romantic intent on saving man by giving him back the *piazza*.

Several other contributions to the development of a satisfactory theory of architectural space could be mentioned, and the particular ideas of Robert Venturi, Aldo van Eyck, Paolo Portoghesi and others will be returned to later. For the moment, however, let us take a brief look at recent thinking about space in general.

From what has been said above, it is clear that further research on architectural space is dependent upon a better understanding of existential space. To arrive at such an understanding, we have two possible sources of information: the social sciences and philosophy. Although the social sciences have scarcely studied the problem of existential space as such, a great deal can be inferred from the writings of certain psychologists, sociologists and anthropologists. In particular, Jean Piaget's work on the development of the child illuminates the basic structures of man's environmental image very clearly. It is also significant that Piaget, in a recent book, integrates the psychological structures in a more comprehensive 'structuralism'.[34]

Several fundamental studies on space have been published by philosophers. Most important are Gaston Bachelard *The Poetics of Space* (1964). Otto Friedrich Bollnow *Mensch und Raum* (1963), the chapter on space in Merleau-Ponty *The Phenomenology of Perception* (1962) and above all the funda-

29 D. Frey *Grundlegung zu einer vergleichenden Kunstwissenschaft* 1949, p. 6

30 Already in *Gotik und Renaissance als Grundlagen der modernen Weltanschauung* (1929) Frey recognized the importance of the 'image', saying, 'The basis of a cultural history is a history of the development of human imagination.'

31 R. Schwarz *The Church Incarnate* 1958; *Von der Bebauung der Erde* 1949

32 K. Lynch *The Image of the City* 1960, p. 4

33 K. Lynch *The Image of the City* 1960, p. 7

34 J. Piaget *Le Structuralisme* 1968

35   See also E. Minkowski *Le temps vécu* 1933 and Graf K. von Dürckheim 'Untersuchungen sum gelebten Raum' *Neue Psychologische* Studien 6 1932

36   M. Merleau-Ponty *The Phenomenology of Perception* 1962, p. 256

37   M. Merleau-Ponty *The Phenomenology of Perception* 1962, p. 285

38   M. Merleau-Ponty *The Phenomenology of Perception* 1962, p. 293

39   M. Heidegger 'Bauen Wohnen Denken' p. 31

40   M. Heidegger *Being and Time* 1962, p. 103

41   M. Heidegger 'Bauen Wohnen Denken' 1954, p. 29

42   M. Heidegger 'Bauen Wohnen Denken' 1954, p. 32

43   M. Heidegger 'Bauen Wohnen Denken' 1954, p. 35

44   Graf K. von Dürckheim 'Untersuchungen zum gelebten Raum' 1932, p. 389; O. F. Bollnow *Mensch und Raum* 1963, p. 20

45   C. Norberg-Schulz *Intentions in Architecture* 1963, p. 97

mental pioneer works of Martin Heidegger *Being and Time* (translated 1962) and 'Bauen Wohnen Denken' (in *Vorträge und Aufsätze* 1954).[35] Merleau-Ponty criticizes the superficiality of certain theories of perception psychology and demonstrates that 'the "signs" (*cues*) which ought to acquaint us with the experience of space can convey the idea of space only if they are already involved in it, and if it is already known'. He concludes: ' . . . depth is the most "existential" of all dimensions'.[36] Later he discusses the existential meaning of place and direction on the basis that 'there is a determining of up and down, and in general of place, which precedes "perception" . . . I arrive in a village for my holidays, and it becomes the centre of my life . . . Our body and our perception always summon us to take as the centre of the world that environment with which they present us. But this environment is not necessarily that of our own life. I can be somewhere else while staying here.'[37] For Merleau-Ponty, space is one of the structures which express our 'being in the world': 'We have said that space is existential; we might just as well have said that existence is spatial'.[38]

Merleau-Ponty, as well as Bachelard and Bollnow, obviously owes much to Heidegger, who was the first to maintain that 'existence is spatial'. 'You cannot divorce man and space. Space is neither an external object nor an internal experience. We don't have man and space besides . . .'[39] In *Being and Time* he is already stressing the existential character of human space and says: 'The "above" is what is "on the ceiling"; the "below" is what is "on the floor"; the "behind" is what is "at the door"; all "wheres" are discovered and circumspectly interpreted as we go our ways in everyday dealings; they are not ascertained and catalogued by the observational measurement of space.'[40] He therefore concludes: 'Spaces receive their being from places and not from "the space".'[41] On this basis he develops his theory of 'dwelling' and says: 'Man's relation to places and through places to spaces consist in dwelling.'[42] 'Only when we are capable of dwelling can we build.' 'Dwelling is the *essential property* of existence.'[43]

Bollnow discusses similar ideas in more detail, and develops a comprehensive theory of existential space, with numerous references to architectural space. He quotes Graf von Dürckheim to define his aim:

'The concrete space of developed man must be considered in its totality, including the important events experienced within it. For the particular quality of this space, its disposition and order reflect and express the subject that experiences it and dwells within it.'[44]

Starting from this point Bollnow discusses the concept of place (*Ort*), basic orientations such as vertical and horizontal, before and behind, right and left, the concept of centre (*Mitte*), geographical directions, horizon and perspective. He goes on to investigate the phenomenology of 'open' and 'closed' worlds, and finally discusses the spaces of action, of expression, and of human being together. He concludes with a chapter on the 'spatiality of human life'. Being speculative rather than scientific, Bollnow's work has been met with a certain suspicion. His material, however, is very rich, drawing its references from nature, literature, art, history, anthropology, psychology and philosophy. His arguments are weighty and substantial, and create a most inspiring basis for further research.

The aim of this chapter has been to outline the basic space concepts man needs to orient himself in his world and to point out that most studies of architectural space have hitherto been hampered by imprecise conceptual definitions and the omission of the key construct, 'existential space'. In *Intentions in Architecture* (1963) I maintained that the space concept is of limited importance in architectural theory, and concluded that 'there is no reason to let the word "space" designate anything but the tridimensionality of any building'.[45] This stand was based on the fact that studies of geometry or visual perception only grasp relatively superficial aspects of the problem. By introducing the concept of existential space, however, these limitations are overcome, and space regains the central position it ought to have in architectural theory.

2 Existential space

The Vale of Blackmoor was to her the world, and its inhabitants the races thereof. From the gates and stiles of Marlott she had looked down its length in the wondering days of infancy, and what had been a mystery to her then was not much less than mystery to her now. She had seen daily from her chamber-window towers, villages, faint white mansions; above all the town of Shaston standing majestically on its height; its windows shining like lamps in the evening sun. She had hardly ever visited the place, only a small tract even of the Vale and its environs being known to her by close inspection. Much less had she been far outside the valley. Every contour of the surrounding hills was as personal to her as that of her relatives' faces; but for what lay beyond her judgment was dependent on the teaching of the village school. . . .

Thomas Hardy *Tess of the d'Urbervilles*

The elements of existential space

We have defined existential space as a relatively stable system of perceptual schemata, or 'image' of the environment. Being a generalization abstracted from the similarities of many phenomena, existential space has 'object-character'.[1] Piaget says: 'An object is a system of perceptual images endowed with a constant spatial form throughout its sequential displacements and constituting an item which can be isolated in the causal series unfolding in time'.[2] He demonstrates that the idea of a structured world gradually develops during childhood (perhaps on the basis of a few *a priori* intuitions), and that, necessarily, it comprises a developing series of spatial notions. How, then, does this development take place? Piaget usually characterizes the process with the word 'conservation'. The most basic experience is that things are *permanent*, although they may disappear and return again. The goal is 'the construction of permanent objects under the moving images of immediate perception'.[3] This means, firstly, that the child learns to *recognize*, that is, to construct the world as a system of similarities, and, secondly, that he connects the things recognized with particular *places*, situating them in a more comprehensive totality, a *space*. 'So long as the child does not undertake special searches to find objects which disappear, so long as he does not succeed in deducing their displacement

in space when he no longer sees them, one should not yet speak of object conservation.'[4] Gradually the child learns, however, to distinguish between stable and mobile objects, and to use the former as a frame of reference for the latter. The development of the concept of place, and of space as a system of places is therefore a necessary condition for finding an existential foothold. Piaget concludes: 'The universe is built up into an aggregate of permanent objects connected by causal relations that are independent of the subject and are placed in space and time. Such a universe, instead of depending on personal activity, is on the contrary imposed upon the self to the extent that it comprises the organism as a part in a whole.'[5] As to the nature of space he says: ' . . . the true nature of space does not reside in the more or less extended character of sensations as such, but in the intelligence which interconnects these sensations'.[6] 'Space is therefore the product of an interaction between the organism and the environment in which it is impossible to dissociate the organization of the universe perceived from that of the activity itself.'[7]

But it is not enough to point out that space forms a necessary part of the structure of existence, we ought also to *describe* this particular structure in detail. The problem comprises two aspects, one 'abstract' and one 'concrete'. The abstract aspect consists

1 C. Norberg-Schulz *Intentions in Architecture* 1963, p. 28

2 J. Piaget *The Child's Construction of Reality* 1955, p. 92

3 J. Piaget *The Child's Construction of Reality* 1955, p. 91

4 J. Piaget *The Child's Construction of Reality* 1955, p. 90

5 J. Piaget *The Child's Construction of Reality* 1955, pp. 351f

6 J. Piaget *The Child's Construction of Reality* 1955, p. 212

7 J. Piaget *The Child's Construction of Reality* 1955, p. 217

8 C. Norberg-Schulz
Intentions in Architecture
1963, pp. 43ff., also Piaget
and Inhelder *The Child's
Conception of Space* 1960

9 M. Wertheimer 'Laws
of Organization in
Perceptual Forms', *A
Source Book of Gestalt
Psychology* (ed W. D.
Ellis) 1938

10 M. Eliade *Patterns in
Comparative Religion* 1958,
p. 380

of the more general schemata of a topological or geometrical kind, and has been studied by Piaget in detail. The concrete aspect refers rather to the grasping of 'environmental elements': landscape, townscape, buildings and physical things, and has been discussed in the works of Frey, Schwarz, Bachelard, Bollnow and Lynch. A theory of existential space must comprise both.

The world of the child is 'subjectively centred'. Motorically and perceptually a child has little ability to 'reach out' into the surroundings, and the environmental image consists of few stable elements. But this does not mean that a child's world is different from the world of other individuals. Psychologists have shown that the elementary structures are interpersonal, and that the development of schemata follows a normal course. Piaget thus demonstrates that the infant's space can be described as a collection of separate 'spaces', each entirely centred on a single activity. The first relations which bring order into these spaces, are of a topological kind and are established even before form- and size-constancy. Topology does not deal with permanent distances, angles and areas, but is based upon relations such as proximity, separation, succession, closure (inside-outside) and continuity.[8] The topological schemata are in the beginning tied to the things themselves. The most elementary order obtained is based on the proximity relation, but the 'collection' thus established, soon develops into more structured wholes, characterized by continuity and enclosure.[9] Piaget's findings are here in accordance with Gestalt psychology, although he gives the organizational principles a different, genetic explanation. If we want to interpret these basic results of perception psychology in more general terms, we may say that the elementary organizational schemata consist in the establishment of *centres* or places (proximity), *directions* or paths (continuity) and *areas* or domains (enclosure). To orient himself, man above all needs to grasp such relations, whereas the geometrical schemata develop much later, to serve more particular purposes. In fact, primitive man mostly manages very well without any geometric notions.

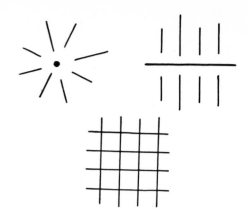

It is of fundamental importance to recognize that the topological schemata are similar to the basic concepts established by Heidegger, Frey, Schwarz, Bollnow and Lynch. The elementary properties of existential space, therefore, seem to be quite clear, and ought to be discussed in more detail.

Centre and place

In terms of spontaneous perception, man's space is 'subjectively centred'. The development of schemata, however, does not only mean that the notion of centre is established as a means of general organization, but that certain centres are 'externalized' as points of reference in the environment. This need is so strong that man since remote times has thought of the whole world as being centralized. In many legends the 'centre of the world' is concretized as a tree or a pillar symbolizing a vertical *axis mundi*. Mountains were also looked upon as points where sky and earth meet.[10] The ancient Greeks

placed the 'navel' of the world (*omphalos*) in Delphi, while the Romans considered their Capitol as *caput mundi*. For Islam the *Ka'aba* is still the centre of the world. Eliade points out that in most beliefs it is *difficult* to reach the centre. It is an ideal goal, which one can only attain after a 'hard journey'. To 'reach the centre is to achieve a consecration, an initiation. To the profane and illusory existence of yesterday, there succeeds a new existence, real, lasting and powerful.' But Eliade also points out that 'every life, even the least eventful, can be taken as the journey through a labyrinth. The sufferings and trials undergone by Ulysses were fabulous, and yet any man's return home has the value of Ulysses' return to Ithaca.'[11]

If the 'centre of the world' thus designates an ideal, public goal, or 'lost paradise', the word 'home' also has a closer and more concrete meaning. It simply tells us that any man's personal world has its centre. The *Odyssey*, however, shows that the home, too, is easily lost and that it takes a 'hard

journey' to find it again. The notion of home as the centre of one's world goes back to childhood. The first points of reference are tied to the home and house, and the child only becomes able to cross its borders very slowly. When I once asked my twelve-year-old son if he could tell me something about his 'environment', he replied: 'Then I want to start with home, because it is from there I go out to all the other places'. From the very beginning, then, the centre represents to man what is *known* in contrast to the unknown and somewhat frightening world around. 'It is the point where he acquires position as a thinking being in space, the point where he "lingers" and "lives" in the space.'[12] We also remember Archimedes' famous statement: 'Give me a place to stand, and I will move the world!'

During growth the actions of the individual are differentiated and multiplied, and new centres therefore come to supplement the original 'home'. All the centres are 'places of

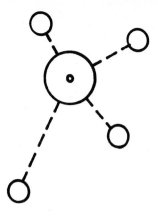

action': places where particular activities are carried out, or places of social interaction such as the homes of relatives and friends. 'The place is always limited, it has been created by man and set up for his special purpose.'[13] The actions, in fact, are only meaningful in relation to particular places, and are coloured by the character of the place. Our language expresses this state of affairs when we say that something 'takes place'. The places are goals or foci where we experience the meaningful events of our existence, but they are also points of departure from which we orient ourselves and take possession of the environment. This 'taking possession' is also related to places which we *expect* to find, or *discover* by surprise. It could be maintained that the gradual multiplication of the places constituting our existential place would lead to a final liberation from place attachment. We will discuss the problem of 'mobility' in more detail later, but should point out here that a structured environment depends on our ability to *recognize* it, that is, on the existence of relatively invariant places. An ever-changing world would not allow for the establishment of schemata, and would therefore make human development impossible.

A place is characterized by a certain 'size'. We should here distinguish between the immediate *Eigenraum* or 'territoriality', and the more abstract image of the places known. The *Eigenraum* has been studied by Edward T. Hall who says: 'Territoriality is usually defined as the behaviour by which an organism characteristically lays claim to an

11 M. Eliade *Patterns in Comparative Religion* 1958, p. 382

12 O. F. Bollnow *Mensch und Raum* 1963, p. 58

13 O. F. Bollnow *Mensch und Raum* 1963, p. 41

14   E. T. Hall *The Hidden Dimension* 1966, ch. 1 and 2. See also R. Sommer *Personal Space* 1969

15   R. Schwarz *Von der Bebauung der Erde* 1949, p. 194

16   O. F. Bollnow *Mensch und Raum* 1963, p. 131

17   K. Jaspers *Von der Wahrheit* Munich 1947, p. 50

18   R. Schwarz *Vom Bau der Kirche* (*The Church Incarnate*) pp. 24ff. (author's own translation)

area and defends it against members of its own species . . . Territoriality provides the frame in which things are done – places to learn, places to play, safe places to hide . . . Basic to territoriality is a sharp sense of the limits that mark the distance to be maintained between individuals.'[14] The 'personal space' defined in the concept of 'territoriality' should not, however, be confounded with existential space, which to a large extent has a 'public' character, bringing the members of a society together in *common* places. Within this public space the individual finds his personal place. Both are generally imagined as being limited and relatively small. Thus Rudolf Schwarz says: 'A domain can only become a home if it is small . . . The settlements must remain within an imaginable scale if they are to become a home.'[15] Bollnow uses the word *Geborgenheit* to express this fact, and quotes the psychiatrist J. Zutt who has studied the concept of 'home' from a medical point of view. Zutt says: 'In the common dwelling we have a maximum of spatial security.'[16] For its definition therefore, the place needs a pronounced limit or border. The place is experienced as an 'inside' in contrast to the surrounding 'outside'.

The limited size of known places naturally goes together with a centralized form. A centralized form primarily means 'concentration'. A place, therefore, is basically 'round'. In this connection it is interesting to recall Karl Jaspers' words: 'In itself every existence appears round.'[17] The round form consists of two elements, a centre and a surrounding ring. In *The Church Incarnate* Rudolf Schwarz has described the existential character of these elements.

'The ring unites man to man through the infinite chain of hands. The individual is absorbed by a superior form, and thereby he becomes stronger. When men agree, they form a ring, as if they were following a secret law. The ring has neither beginning nor end, it begins and ends everywhere. Curved back into itself, it is the most sincere and potent of all figures, the most unanimous. Hand in hand men are united by the ring, but they are not completely absorbed by this

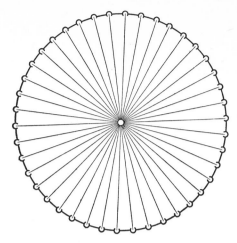

attachment. Their eyes are free. Through the eyes life goes out, and returns saturated with reality. The eyes are brought together in the centre as the common focus. Thereby the fellowship attains a stricter form. Everyone is still open to the inside, but only completely open to the central point. In this point men are united. But not in such a way that the individual becomes lonely; rather, he knows that the real road inwards, to the hearts of the others, goes through the centre. The meeting now becomes a meeting in the common centre of meaning. Between the centre and the ring a star is formed, through which men transmit their existence to the world around.'[18]

The notions of proximity, centralization and closure therefore work together to form a more concrete existential concept, the concept of *place*, and places are the basic elements of existential space.

Direction and path

I have already pointed out that the concept of place implies an inside and an outside, and that existential space usually comprises many places. A place is therefore 'situated' within a larger context, and cannot be understood in isolation. If that had been possible, man's history would have lacked its dynamism. Any place, in fact, contains *directions*. The only place that can be imagined without directions, is a sphere freely floating in

Euclidean space. This form, however, is only of interest as a border-line case, if we consider man's existence on earth.[19] The semi-sphere already expresses the basic difference between the horizontal and vertical directions in existential space.

Aristotle recognized the qualitative distinctions above and below, in front of and behind, and right and left, distinctions which are rooted in man's constitution and in his relationship to the gravitational field. The vertical direction expresses a rising up or falling down, and has since remote times been endowed with a particular meaning. Erich Kästner says:

'The climbing of a mountain reflects redemption. That is due to the force of the word "above", and the power of the word "up". Even those who have long ceased to believe in Heaven and Hell, cannot exchange the words "above" and "below".'[20]

The vertical, therefore, has always been considered the *sacred* dimension of space. It represents a 'path' towards a reality which may be 'higher' or 'lower' than daily life, a reality which conquers gravity, that is, earthly existence, or succumbs to it. The *axis mundi* is thus more than the centre of the world, it represents a connection between the three cosmic realms, and it is only at the central axis that a breakthrough from one realm to another can occur.[21]

The vertical direction, however, also has a more concrete meaning. In connection with the home it expresses the very process of *building*, that is, man's ability to 'conquer nature'. In Ibsen's play *The Master Builder* the tower becomes the symbol of victory and defeat, and Serlio already interpreted the vertical column as an expression of man's power of creation.[22] Gaston Bachelard defines the basic properties of the house as 'verticality' and 'concentration', and he discusses the cellar and the attic as particularly meaningful places.[23] Quoting Joe Bosquet he also characterizes modern man as 'having one storey only'.

If verticality has something surreal about it,

the horizontal directions represent man's concrete world of action. In a certain sense, all horizontal directions are equal and form a plane of infinite extension. The simplest model of man's existential space is, therefore, a horizontal plane pierced by a vertical axis. But on the plane man chooses and

creates paths which give his existential space a more particular structure. Man's taking possession of the environment always means a departure from the place where he dwells, and a journey along a path which leads him in a direction determined by his purpose and his image of the environment. 'Forward', thus, means the direction of man's activity, while 'behind' denotes the distance he has covered. Man 'strides forward' or 'draws back'. Sometimes the path leads him to a known goal, but often it only indicates an intended direction, gradually dissolving into the unknown distance. The *path*, therefore, represents a basic property of human existence, and it is one of the great

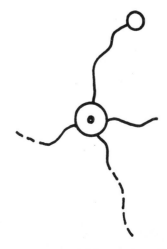

19 It is interesting to notice that the sphere appears in architectural projects to express a 'liberation from place'. See H. Sedlmayr *Art in Crisis* 1957. Sedlmayr uses the term 'das Bodenlose' (foundationless) to characterize the spherical projects of Ledoux, Boullée and Tatlin. He quotes El Lissitzky, 'One of our ideas for the future is to overcome the foundation, to no longer be earthbound'.

20 E. Kästner *Ölberge, Weinberge* 1960, p. 95

21 M. Eliade *Patterns in Comparative Religion* 1958, p. 111

22 O. F. Bollnow *Mensch und Raum* p. 171 says, 'By standing up man gains stature in the world, he is enabled to keep his independence vis à vis the world and he can shape the world and himself. Going to sleep means abandoning the position . . . as we lie down to sleep, stretch out, we give ourselves over totally to the world . . .'

23 Bachelard *The Poetics of Space* 1964 ch. I

24 Particularly significant are the German words 'Scheideweg', 'Worsicht' and 'Fortschritt' – literally 'dividing ways' (i.e. crossroads), 'foresight' (i.e. caution), 'away step' (i.e. progress)

25 O. F. Bollnow *Mensch und Raum* 1963, p. 81

26 E. Cassirer *The Philosophy of Symbolic Forms* 1955, vol 2, p. 99

27 W. Müller *Die heilige Stadt* 1961, p. 16

28 R. Schwarz *Von der Bebauung der Erde* 1949, p. 15

29 K. Lewin 'Der Richtungsbegriff in der Psychologie. Der spezielle und allgemeine hodologische Raum *Psychologische Forschung* 19, 1934

30 K. Lewin says, 'The geometry of *Lebensraum* including its directions depends on the condition of the individual.' (*op cit.*, p. 286)

31 O. F. Bollnow *Mensch und Raum* 1963, p. 197

original symbols. Our language expresses this fact in terms such as 'parting of the ways', 'stand in one's way' and 'on the right road'.[24] Man's ways, however, also lead back home, and the path, therefore, always contains a tension between the known and the unknown. 'The double movement of departure and return divides space into two concentric domains, an inner and an outer: the narrower inner is the domain of the house and homeland and from there man advances into the wider outer domain, from which he also returns.'[25]

The directions of existential space, however, are not only determined by man's actions. Nature, too, contains directions which indicate qualitative differences. Thus the

cardinal points have since remote times been given prime importance among the factors determining the structure of the world. The word 'orientation' comes from *Orient*, the direction of sunrise. Christian churches were always oriented by the altar towards the east. 'The east as the origin of light is also the source of life – the west as the place of the setting sun is filled with all the terrors of death.'[26] In certain theories the cardinal points were united with the *axis mundi* to form a comprehensive cosmology. Vitruvius says that 'Nature has put one *cardo* of the world axis through a northern point behind the Great Bear, and the other under the earth to the opposite regions in the south.'[27] The Roman city, thus, was organized around the *cardo* (*axis mundi*) running north-south and the *decumanus* running east-west. 'He founds his city by tracing on the land two crossing roads which divide the world as a compass in four, and he then surrounds this central juncture with walls.'[28]

Nature also determines the directions of man's existential space in a more concrete sense. Any landscape contains directions as well as determined spaces which help man in finding a foothold. His possibilities for movement are limited, and the paths do not follow the mathematical rule that the shortest distance is the straight line. In an early essay, Kurt Lewin studied this problem introducing the term 'hodological space' (from the Greek word *hodos* meaning way),[29] which could be translated into 'space of possible movement'. Rather than straight lines, hodological space contains 'preferred paths' which represent a compromise between several domains such as 'short distance', 'security', 'minimal work', 'maximum experience' etc. The demands are determined in relation to the topographical conditions. When these are uniform, and no particular human activity influences the situation, hodological space approaches Euclidean space. In hodological space, however, we usually have to follow directions which do not correspond to the geometrical direction towards the goal, and investigations of people's movement in cities show that different individuals often chose different paths to reach the same place.[30] Bollnow also points out that the preferred path of an individual may vary according to his immediate state of mind, or situation. We will, for instance, take a short cut when we are in a hurry.[31]

Perceptually and as a schema, any path is characterized by its *continuity*. Whereas the place is determined by the proximity of its defining elements, and eventually by closure, the path is imagined as a linear succession. Primarily it is a direction to be followed towards a goal, but during the journey events happen and the path is also experienced as having a character of its own. What happens 'along' the way, thus, is added to the tension created by the goal to be reached and the point of departure left behind. In certain

32 K. Lynch *The Image of the City* 1960, p. 54

33 W. Müller *Die heilige Stadt* 1961, p. 38

34 W. Müller *Die heilige Stadt* 1961, p. 227

cases the path has the function of being an organizing *axis* for the elements by which it is accompanied, while the goal is relatively less important. Kevin Lynch illustrates this fact with many examples, but he also says: 'People tended to think of path destinations and origin points: they liked to know where paths came from and where they led. Paths with clear and well known origins and destinations had stronger identities, helped tie the city together, and gave the observer a sense of his bearings whenever he crossed them.'[32]

Area and domain

Paths divide man's environment into areas which are more or less well known. We will call such qualitatively defined areas 'domains'. The known domains are surrounded by a relatively unknown world whose imagined character is determined by the general directions north, south, east and west and by what we have learnt of geography. In a certain sense the domains are

'places', because they are defined by closure or by proximity and similarity of the constituent elements. For this reason Frey and others do not introduce the concept of domain, but describe space exclusively in terms of goals and paths. But the distinction between place and domain *is* useful, as our environmental image obviously comprises areas to which we do *not* belong and which do not function as goals. The domain can therefore be defined as a relatively unstructured 'ground', on which places and paths appear as more pronounced 'figures'. The domain

has a certain unifying function in existential space. It 'fills out' the image and makes it become a coherent space. If we think of our own country, or of the earth as a whole, we primarily think of domains: oceans, deserts, mountains and lakes, which form a continuous mosaic. These 'natural' domains are combined with political and economical domains to create a more complex pattern.

Because of their general properties, domains function as potential places for man's activities. Taking possession of the environment, therefore, implies structuring the environment into domains by means of paths and places. The Roman settlement is again relevant, where the two main axes not only define the cardinal points, but also divide the

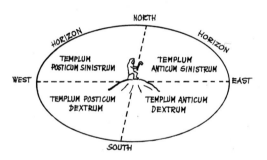

area into four domains or 'quarters'. It is significant to remember that city districts are still called quarters. From ancient times the world was imagined as consisting of four parts, and the Roman city can thus be interpreted as an *imago mundi*. The rituals performed during the foundation of any larger Roman layout, demonstrate that the purpose was to define a comprehensive spatial order related to a central point.[33] This order was established within the natural area defined by the horizon, the *finalis circulus*. Werner Müller discusses the ancient symbolism of dividing the world into domains and explains the idea as an expression of man's general need for imagining his world 'as an ordered cosmos within an unordered chaos'.[34]

Structuring the world into domains defined by 'natural' directions, ancient man gained an existential foothold. He no longer felt

35 K. Lynch *The Image of the City* 1960, p. 62

36 O. Spengler *The Decline of the West* 1934, vol 1, p. 188

lost and helpless, as even the 'blank spots' on his personal map could be 'placed' within the general all-embracing scheme. Modern man, however, can no longer find the same security. He asks for a concrete knowledge of individual places, rather than accepting general 'characteristics'. When we are travelling in foreign countries, the regions we visit have relatively little meaning for us. No personal experiences are attached to the spaces perceived and they really remain 'domains', although as such they may interest the visitor. Today we are no longer able to make up for this lack of deeper meaning with a cosmological image which gives each domain its character. Paradoxically, thus, the foreign has become more foreign today, in spite of all modern media of communication.

Domains may be defined in different ways. Sometimes they are delimited by strong natural elements, such as shore lines, rivers and hills, called 'edges' by Kevin Lynch who says: 'Edges are the linear elements not considered as paths: they are usually, but not always, the boundaries between two kinds of areas'.[35] Sometimes domains are defined by the particular human activities carried out in the area, such as agriculture or dwelling, which create a certain 'texture'. Social conditions may also determine a domain's character, as the east- and west-ends of many cities show. Often different factors come together to reinforce the image of distinct domains. On a larger scale, even climate creates distinguishable domains which are experienced as such. Modern topoclimatology also illustrates that there are smaller climatically defined domains which we are hardly aware of, but which have evidently been recognized by man during history as factors determining the distribution of areas for agriculture and housing. It is therefore clear that man's image of domains is influenced by physical and functional as well as social and cultural factors, that is, by the basic objects to which he has to orient.

Elementary interaction

Places, paths and domains are the basic schemata of orientation, that is, the con-stituent elements of existential space. When they are combined space becomes a real dimension of human existence. It has already been pointed out that the character of a place must be understood as a product of its interaction with the surroundings; that a path without a goal becomes rather meaningless; and that domains, finally, function as a less structured, but unifying 'ground'. The elements can be combined in several ways. The existential space of nomadic

people gives primary importance to the domain within which the paths have a great range of freedom, but their place concept is less developed. Early agricultural civilizations were 'place-oriented', living a static life within a centralized, 'closed' area. Their paths have a circular, engirdling movement, rather than functioning as a direction towards a goal outside. In ancient Egypt, however, the path was the basic symbol.

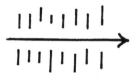

'The Egyptian soul saw itself as moving down a narrow and inexorably-prescribed life-path to come at the end before the judges of the dead. That was its *Destiny-idea*.'[36] Even the Egyptian 'domain', the long and narrow oasis of the Nile valley, can by its very nature be defined as a 'path'. In later civilizations the three elements entered in ever new meaningful combinations. An analysis of existential space, therefore, ought to start investigating the relative importance given to each of the basic elements. Thereafter the interaction of the elements should be studied.

When places interact with their surroundings, a problem of *inside* and *outside* is created.[37] This topological relation, therefore, is a fundamental aspect of existential space. 'To be inside' is, obviously, the

37 For a more detailed discussion of open and closed forms see Norberg-Schulz *Intentions in Architecture* 1963, pp. 136ff

38 For a discussion of the existential aspects of the inside-outside relationship see Bachelard *The Poetics of Space* 1964, ch IX

39 O. F. Bollnow *Mensch und Raum* 1963, p. 154

primary intention behind the place concept, that is, to be somewhere, away from what is 'outside'. Only when man has defined what is inside and what is outside, can we really say that he 'dwells'. Through this attachment, man's experiences and memories are located, and the inside of space becomes an expression of the 'inside' of personality.[38] 'Identity', thus, is closely connected with the experience of place, especially during the years when personality is shaped. To function as an inside a place obviously has to satisfy certain formal demands. We have already quoted Rudolf Schwarz's description of the ring as a maximally 'closed' form, and could add that the closure may be increased through geometrization, that is,

by making the ring circular. Geometrization, in general, does away with all the casual directions of the topological form, and has always been used by man to make the intended relationship more precise.

Any closed form, however, has to be *entered*, and a direction is thereby introduced. 'For a house not to become a prison it must have openings into the world beyond, that connect this inner world with the outer.'[39] The direction unites inside and outside more or less strongly, and we see again that a geometrically straight line is more powerful than a topological curve. The place as such is also influenced by the direction; it is 'stretched' towards the outside, at the same time as the outside penetrates the border,

creating an area of transition. This area is related to an *opening* which may be given various forms to express the degree of continuity in existential space. No wonder, therefore, that the door since remote times has been one of the important symbolic elements of architecture. The door can close off or open up, it can unite and separate. Psychologically it is always open and closed *at the same time* although one aspect is dominating, as any door may be opened. The opening is the element that makes the place become alive, because the basis of any life is interaction with an environment. A single opening in an enclosure, however, does not take the cardinal points into consideration. Being part of a natural context the place is already 'oriented', and the ancient city which was divided into quarters symbolized a fourfold 'opening', which made the city a part of the surrounding world. In general, the opening expresses what the place 'wants to be' in relation to its environment.

A place is usually related to several directions by a system of paths; these often form a 'star' around the centre. As the paths are

40 O. F. Bollnow *Mensch und Raum* 1963, p. 100

41 M. Heidegger 'Bauen Wohnen Denken 1954, p. 26

42 See H. Dittmar *Der Kampf der Kathedralen* 1964

determined by related human activities which form a coherent action-pattern, the paths are usually connected among themselves. The result is a network which may be

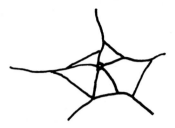

more or less uniform and geometrical, according to the type of activities and the topographical conditions.[40] Some paths are experienced as such because they lead to significant places, whereas others (which lead to the places of other individuals) are only known as a characteristic textural feature of a domain. Holland is a good example of a country which is easily imagined because of its regular path system.

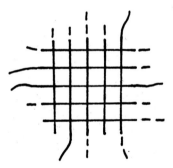

The Dutch countryside, in fact, is divided to form regular grids, because of the system of reclaiming land from the sea, or 'polders'. When two paths meet several expressive solutions are possible on the basis of the continuity principle. We may have a 'bifurcation' or a 'crossroads', both of which have strong existential implications. The choice,

in fact, is a basic problem of human life, especially when posed as a choice between which direction to take to reach a more or less clearly imagined goal. The 'bridge' is a particularly expressive path. Joining two domains and containing two directions, it is usually in a strongly felt state of dynamic equilibrium. Heidegger says: 'Bridges assemble the earth as landscape around the river.'[41] The system of paths, therefore, expresses man's possibilities of movement, the range of his world. We here return to Lewin's hodological space, a concept which ought to be revived and further developed.

The relation between place and path creates a basic dichotomy, which has been strongly felt by European man throughout history. We may call it 'the tension between centralization and longitudinality'. Whereas centralization symbolizes the need for belonging to a place, the longitudinal movement expresses a certain openness to the world, a dynamism which may be physical as well as spiritual. Whereas centralization has ancient roots in the Orient, where it expresses the idea of an 'eternal return', longitudinality was introduced by the Jews who imagined life as a 'path'. The Bible, in fact, states the theme clearly with its opening words: 'In the *beginning* God created Heaven and Earth . . .'. When beginning and end are distinguished, the continuous (and possibly straight) line becomes the appropriate spatial counterpart. In ancient Rome the two images were brought together, and later remained linked, although centralization was to dominate the world image of Eastern Europe and longitudinality the more dynamic intentions of the West.[42]

The system of paths, together with the topographical conditions, creates domains of varying 'density' in our environmental image. The domains with a higher density will be experienced as 'shapes', whereas the

lower densities define a more neutral 'ground'. This simply means that we know the denser areas better, because physically or intellectually we have 'conquered' them by means of more paths. The denser areas thus become places, although they may not have a clearly defined boundary, whereas the other areas remain domains. This aspect of the problem is mentioned to stress that human identification with the environment presupposes *varying* densities, and above all, dense foci which serve as basic points of reference.

The environmental image is therefore composed of a few basic elements, which interact in characteristic ways. In the next section this interaction will be discussed in more detail, and interpreted in human and cultural terms. But to conclude this elementary part of the theory of existential space, we will recall the old concept of *genius loci*. Since remote times man has recognized that diff-

erent places have a different character. This character is often so strong that it in fact determines the basic properties of the environmental images of most people present, making them feel that they experience and belong to the same place. The *genius loci* in many cases has even proved strong enough to dominate any political, social and cultural changes. This, for instance, holds true for cities like Rome, Istanbul, Paris, Prague and Moscow.[43] Indeed, the truly 'great' city is characterized by a particularly pronounced *genius loci*. I want to point to this fact to stress that existential space cannot be understood in terms of man's *needs* alone, but only as a result of his *interaction* with an environment, which he has to understand and accept. In this way we return to Piaget's double concept of assimilation and accommodation. Existential space, therefore, symbolizes man's *being in the world*, or in Heidegger's words: 'Das Dasein ist räumlich'.[44]

43 See C. Norberg-Schulz 'Möte med Istanbul' *Byggekunst* 1967, p. 104

44 M. Heidegger *Being and Time* 1962, p. 146

The levels of existential space

So far the basic schemata which form the elements of existential space have been discussed. If we look upon the problem in a more concrete way, we find that the elements appear on several levels within a hierarchy of which the most comprehensive are levels of 'geography' and landscape, while at the opposite end of the hierarchy is an order of furniture and still smaller objects. The levels are determined by the given environment as well as by man's constitution. It would, in fact, be wrong to imagine our environment as being 'continuous'. Certain sizes of spatial units are simply of no use, or if they are produced, have an illusory and amusing effect.[1] The lowest level is determined by the *hand*. The sizes and shapes of articles for use are related to the functions of grasping, carrying and in general of extending the actions of the hand. The next level, furniture, is determined by the size of the *body*, especially in relation to such activities as sitting, bending and lying down.

The third level, the house, gets its dimensions from the more extended bodily *movements* and actions, as well as from 'territorial' demands. The urban level (which comprises sub-levels) is mainly determined by *social interaction*, that is, by the common 'form of life'. The landscape level results from man's *interaction with the natural environment*.[2] We can also add still more comprehensive geographical levels, which are developed by travelling from one landscape to another, or on the basis of a general knowledge about the world. The system of levels, the different schemata developed on each level, and the interaction of levels constitute the structure of existential space.

Most civilizations possess all levels, but some of them may be rather undeveloped. Nomadic people, for instance, have little contact with urbanistic schemata, whereas urban people in our time have lost most of the landscape level, although they usually

1 In theatre-decoration, thus, we find 'large furniture' or 'dolls' houses', as well as 'miniature landscapes'. Palladio in his Teatro Olimpico produced a whole townscape behind the stage. Visitors will remember the absurd effect created when a person walks down the 'streets'

2 Needless to say, the determinants on all levels are physical as well as psychic

27

3 Even furniture and objects have in the past been considered images of the world. The chandeliers of the Ottonian and Carolingian epochs, for instance, were images of 'Heavenly Jerusalem'. See H. Sedlmayr *Die Entstehung der Kathedrale* 1950, p. 125

4 P. Haggett *Locational Analysis in Human Geography* 1965, p. 18

5 For the concept of 'capacity' see Norberg-Schulz *Intentions in Architecture* 1963, p. 155

6 R. Schwarz *Von der Bebauung der Erde* 1949, p. 11

7 This fact is expressed by all the names of towns ending with 'ford' (German: *Furt*), meaning 'shallow place where a river may be crossed by wading'

8 See C. Norberg-Schulz 'Möte med Istanbul'

possess some geographical images learnt in school. We will discuss the question of the organization of each level in the following, but should point out in this context that the schemata usually vary from level to level. The house image, for instance, may show a high degree of geometrization, whereas the urban image is topological in character.

Geography

The geographical level has a cognitive character. It is 'thought' rather than 'lived', but may influence the more directly and fully experienced levels. In the past the geographical level hardly existed. Instead we find a 'cosmological' level which was just as real to man as geography is today. We have already mentioned that ancient man conceived his more concrete existential levels as images of the cosmological level.[3] In a certain sense this still happens today, when houses and towns are built on the same Euclidean principles as the space of naïve realism, or when certain works of architecture are inspired by the space-time continuum of relativity. The geographical level, however, hardly serves as a model to be imitated, rather it gives identity to 'objects' such as 'Europe', the 'country' or the 'region', and in so doing assures a considerable political and cultural importance. It also furnishes economical and ecological information which influences man's orientation in the widest sense of the term. The places and paths of geographical space have an abstract character: they do not represent what is directly known, but are *potential* elements of existential space. The content of the geographical level primarily consists of various domains. (In cosmological space the situation is similar, with the difference that the domains symbolize idealized life situations, such as Heaven and Hell.) Peter Haggett, in a fundamental study on geographical theory, uses the concepts of 'network' (i.e. system of routes or paths), 'node', 'surface' (i.e. domain) and 'hierarchy' to describe geographical structure.[4]

Landscape

The level of landscape has generally been

that of the 'ground' on which the configurations of existential space have developed. Strangely, however, man's 'being in the landscape' has hardly been studied. The only coherent theoretical attempt known to us, is found in Rudolf Schwarz's book *Von der Bebauung der Erde*. Obviously the schemata of the landscape level are formed through the interaction of man's activities with topography, vegetation and climate. The same landscape, thus, is in some sense different for the peasant, the miner and the tourist, without, though, becoming entirely different. As any landscape offers a limited range of possibilities for orientation and identification, we may say that it has a certain 'capacity' determined by its structural properties.[5] These structural properties ought to be described in terms of places, paths and domains. Rudolf Schwarz says:

'... we talk about landscape spaces and think of a house; the mountains are walls, the fields floors, the rivers paths, the coasts are edges and the lowest point in the mountain range, the door.'[6]

Although being primarily background, landscape thus has a structure of its own. It offers areas where the development of places is particularly favoured, and it indicates possible paths and natural domains. If we bring together the different human needs which are satisfied by the place concept, we arrive at a formula where identity/security leads to activity. A place is formed where this formula finds its physical counterpart. In concrete terms this means a naturally protected space, which, however, can easily interact with its surroundings. The great cities of the past, therefore, were located on natural paths of communication, such as rivers,[7] at points which offered physical protection as well as a characteristic identity (*genius loci*). In a few cases both demands were satisfied maximally, as for instance in Constantinople-Istanbul, where 'paths' from East and West, North and South meet at a point of incomparable beauty.[8] Landscape obviously also contains potential places which can only satisfy *one* of the basic demands. In such cases the other demand has to be met by artificial means, by planning and building. The formation of paths is also to a large extent determined by natural

28

conditions. Kurt Lewin's idea of the 'preferred path' is confirmed by modern geographical research, where it is pointed out that movement usually follows an optimal path, according to the *lex parsimoniæ*. Deviations from the straight line, however, are usual, either to obtain something ('positive deviation') or to evade an obstacle ('negative deviation').[9] In particular, domains are defined by natural elements. Slopes, edges, variations in texture (vegetation etc.) strongly suggest areas which become part of man's environmental image. Often these areas correspond to those used for a particular purpose, such as agriculture, but mostly the correspondence is not one to one, whereby a wonderful counterpoint between natural and man-made domains results.

But landscape structure, it must be admitted, is in general relatively diffuse. The elements only occasionally have a clear definition, such as a lake, and vegetation and topographical forms rarely correspond exactly. A certain correlation is sometimes found as, for instance, when a cultivated field stops against a wood-clad hill, but regular or geometrical forms hardly exist. When they do occur, man tends to bestow upon them a particular significance: Mount Fuji in Japan is traditionally considered holy, and Vesuvius is even more interesting because of its regular contour, accentuated by the isolated position of the mountain. It would, however, be wrong to consider landscape as formless. A landscape with weak formal properties may exist, but it does not offer the same possibilities for orientation and identification as a landscape where large and small dimensions accentuate each other reciprocally, where masses and spaces inspire us to imagine the experience of taking possession of it by physical and psychic movement. The imagined process of taking possession of landscape during the changing seasons also determines its infinitely varying expressions: it may be intimate or forbidding, smiling or sombre; but all these expressions have a *general* character. As nature is not man-made, it keeps us at a certain distance and offers great but relatively undifferentiated experiences. Correspondingly, the structure of landscape consists of general

topological relationships: we may, for instance, talk about 'a chain of mountains' or 'a glade in the forest'. Let us repeat that landscape always has the function of forming the continuous background of our environmental image (as well as of our visual field). If this condition is corrupted, we stop talking about landscape.[10]

The urban level

On the urban level we find structures which are mostly determined by man's own activities, that is, by his interaction with a *man-made* environment. On this level, therefore, the basic form is what could be called 'our place'. During his development the individual discovers a structured whole which he shares with others and which more than anything else gives him a sense of identity. In fact, during history the town has simply been *civitas*, the known and safe world which secured man's foothold in relation to the unknown world around. The primary quality of the urban image, therefore, is the single identifiable place. To satisfy this condition, the settlement ought to have *figural* character in relation to the landscape. The principles of closure and proximity of the constituent elements, therefore, are of prime importance. The settlement in any case has to have a higher density than its surroundings. This does not mean, however, that the town is a closed system, isolated from its environment. We have already talked about the dialectic of departure and return, of inside and outside and of the meaning of 'openings'. The town, thus, communicates with elements of other levels. But communication presupposes that the town has something to contribute, that is, has a clearly defined identity. Communication does not mean to dissolve into the surroundings.

We have maintained that the identity of a settlement relative to its surroundings depends on a certain density. The question then arises whether this density is also motivated from within. Certainly villages and towns from any period or part of the world were characterized by being dense. This quality, therefore, seems to satisfy a basic

9 P. Haggett *Locational Analysis in Human Geography* 1965, pp. 32, 62ff

10 For a further discussion of the properties of landscape see C. Norberg-Schulz 'Il paesaggio e l'opera dell'uomo' *Edilizia Moderna* 78, 1966

11 See 'Giglio Castello' *Byggekunst* 6/1969

12 A. E. Brinckmann *Deutsche Stadtbaukunst der Vergangenheit* 1911, *Stadtbaukunst* 1920; P. Zucker *Town and Square* 1959

13 C. Lévi-Strauss *Structural Anthropology* 1963, ch. VIII

14 In Appendix A to his book, Lynch refers to rich anthropological material providing further confirmation of the point

15 Lynch *The Image of the City* 1960, p. 41

16 For the concept of 'socialization' see Norberg-Schulz *Intentions in Architecture* 1963, pp. 37ff

17 R. Schwarz *Von der Bebauung der Erde* 1949, pp. 193ff

human need. One might refer to the need for defence, a factor which certainly has played an important role, but density also appears where defence was unnecessary. The motivation, therefore, lies deeper. We know that the Egyptian hieroglyph for 'city' also meant 'mother'. The city was experienced as something close, warm and embracing. When I once asked one of the inhabitants of a small Italian village how she would describe her village to somebody who did not know the place, she answered: 'it is like a warm coat I can put on'.[11] Density thus seems motivated also from within. In general it corresponds to what is usually known as *human scale*.

The discussion of urban structure is not exhausted, however, by pointing out a general place-quality. It also comprises an interior organization which we have already mentioned in connection with the research of Kevin Lynch. Lynch is certainly not the first to define urban structure in terms of 'nodes', 'paths' and 'districts'; conventional descriptions of towns usually refer to squares (*piazza*, *Platz*, *place*), streets and quarters and we may quote the writings of A. E. Brinckmann and Paul Zucker as an example.[12] But he has given these well known terms a new existential dimension, rather than reducing them to aspects of a 'visual' problem. His approach finds significant confirmation in an essay by Claude Lévi-Strauss, who discusses the image natives have of their village.[13] Lévi-Strauss shows that the image is based on simple,

topological relations, but that it varies according to the individual's position in the social structure. He also points out that the image-types correspond to real arrangements found in primitive villages.[14] The inner urban structure is thus a complex result of individual and social functions which 'take place'. The same basic elements are found everywhere; they can, however, be combined into several typical urban images. The most

elementary of these are the 'enclosure' and the 'cluster', which are the direct expressions of functions taking place and of social 'togetherness'. These two structures also often appear in combination, as when a cluster is given a precise delimitation. Continuity along a path is also a characteristic model, mostly determined by particular environmental conditions. In larger cities these structures form hierarchical systems. A higher or lesser degree of geometrization may appear on all sub-levels.

Kevin Lynch uses present-day American cities as his material, but still arrives at the same conclusions. Man needs an urban environment which facilitates the image-making, he needs districts which have a particular character, paths which lead somewhere, and nodes which are 'distinct and unforgettable places'. In his fascinating analysis of formless Los Angeles, he quotes a characteristic statement of one of the persons interviewed: 'It's as if you were going somewhere for a long time, and when you got there you discovered there was nothing there, after all.'[15] Within the urban level, the individual usually possesses his more 'private' existential space, but it is essential that this is understood as part of a larger whole. Such an understanding grows together with man's gradual becoming part of a social context. 'Socialization', thus, has to be accompanied by the development of existential space to become really meaningful.[16] Rudolf Schwarz says: 'The individual is born in the village which existed before him. But slowly this village becomes his homeland, a place lived in and full of memories.' 'Paths and places became memories, time and space became the history of his life.'[17]

The house

The private spaces we find within the common urban level, are *houses* in the fullest sense of the word. The house really brings us inside and represents the need for being situated. But there are also houses which have a public character. This either means that they remain part of the urban level, or that the public realm is recognized as an extension of the private world, so that man can be said to 'dwell' in the public buildings as well as in his own house. In other words, the concept of 'home' may have a varying range. Some forms of life, in fact, give prime importance to the common, public environment; the inhabitants dwell *together* as one large community, whereas elsewhere the house of the *family* is the basic element. In both cases, however, the fundamental function of *dwelling* is fully expressed. Heidegger says:

'What does it mean to build? The old German word for to build was "buan" and means to dwell. That is, to stay, to remain . . . The word "bin" (am) came from the old word to build, so that "I am", "you are" means: I dwell, you dwell. The way that you are and I am, the way men *are* on earth is "Buan", dwelling . . .' 'Dwelling is the basic principle of existence.'[18]

The house, therefore, remains the central place of human existence, the place where the child learns to understand his being in the world, and the place from which man departs and to which he returns. The poet Milosz says:

'I say Mother. And my thoughts are of you, oh, House. House of the lovely dark summers of my childhood.'[19]

and a house-inscription by Hermann Broch reads:

'In der Mitte aller Ferne
steht dies Haus
drum hab es gerne.'[20]

Consequently Gaston Bachelard describes the house as 'one of the great integrative forces in man's life'.[21] In the house man finds his identity.

The structure of the house is primarily that of a place, but as such it also contains an interior structure which is differentiated in several subordinate places and connecting paths. Different activities take place in the house, and their co-ordinate totality expresses a form of life. The activities have a varying relation to the outside and to the basic directions of vertical and horizontal. When Bachelard gives prime importance to the verticality of the house, he obviously recognizes the fundamental relationship discussed by Heidegger: to dwell does not only mean 'to be on earth', but also 'to be under the Heavens'.[22] The house gives man his place on earth, but the 'vertical' is always with him. In general, the house expresses the structure of dwelling, with all its physical and psychic aspects. It is imagined as a system of meaningful activities concretized as a space consisting of places with varying character. To illustrate the depth which is given to the world 'character' in this context, Bachelard quotes C. G. Jung who says: 'Conscience behaves like the man who hearing a suspicious noise in the cellar rushes up to the attic to make sure that there are not thieves and subsequently that the noise was a figment of his imagination. In reality the cautious man hadn't dared to go down to the cellar.'[23] The image of the house, therefore, depends on the existence of differentiated places which interact among themselves and with the environment in varying ways. Above all, however, the character is determined by concrete 'things' such as the fire-place, the table and the bed.

When Alberti called the house 'a small city', he probably felt that we dwell in cities as well as in houses, and that the basic elements of existential space determine both. But the analogy is not completely valid. The house, thus, does not give the same importance to the path as does the city. Whereas the city mainly lives by means of its paths, the house is a function of place. In fact, we can follow a logical progression from the domain-dominated landscape over the path-dominated city to the place-dominated house. At the same time we notice a growing precision of form and structure, that is, an increasing tendency towards geometrization.[24] The more man is 'at home', the more precisely he can define his environment.

The thing

How, then, should we consider the lowest level of existential space, that of furniture and objects-for-use? Here we can no longer talk about a system of places and paths, but

18 M. Heidegger 'Bauen Wohnen Denken' 1954, pp. 20, 21, 35

19 Quoted by G. Bachelard *The Poetics of Space* 1964, ch. II, 4

20 H. Broch *Gedichte* 1953, p. 68.
(In the middle of all distance stands this house, therefore be fond of it)

21 G. Bachelard *The Poetics of Space* 1964, ch. I, 1

22 M. Heidegger 'Bauen Wohnen Denken' 1954, p. 23

23 G. Bachelard *The Poetics of Space* 1964, ch. I, 5

24 This, of course, is not a rule. The Hellenistic town, thus, shows a higher degree of geometrization on the urban level, than in the individual house

25 O. F. Bollnow *Mensch und Raum* 1963, p. 165

26 O. F. Bollnow *Mensch und Raum* 1963, p. 166

27 G. Bachelard *The Poetics of Space* 1964, ch. III, 4

28 G. Bachelard *The Poetics of Space* 1964, ch. III, 6–7

29 For the theory of objects see Norberg-Schulz *Intentions in Architecture* pp. 27ff

30 M. Eliade says, 'The sky directly, "naturally", reveals the infinite distance, the transcendence of the deity'. *The Sacred and the Profane* 1961, p. 117

31 For a discussion of representation see Norberg-Schultz *Intentions in Architecture* 1963, pp. 167ff

are left with *things*, which interact with their surroundings in different ways.[25] Being directly connected with certain functions, 'things' usually have a maximum of precise form, and are known by man in the most direct way possible. We have already mentioned that elements on this level may serve as foci in the house. The fire-place, for instance, has since ancient times been the very centre of the dwelling, and the table was the 'place' where the family joined to form a 'ring'. Bollnow points out that the bed represents the centre even more convincingly, being the place from where man starts his day, and to which he returns in the evening. In bed the circle of the day, and of life, is closed.[26] The bed, therefore, *par excellence* is the place where man 'comes to rest', where his movements find their goal. Bollnow also points out that man's active relationship to the world is characterized by his vertical position; he takes 'a stand'. To sleep means to give up this position and return to the very 'point of departure'. When the Château de Versailles was centralized on the bed of Louis XIV, it symbolized more than a mere demonstration of power. Gaston Bachelard also gives an interpretation of such 'things' as cupboards and drawers. 'In the cupboard,' he says, 'there lives a centre of order, which protects the whole house against chaos.'[27] He points to the fascination we feel when we hear the words 'Open Sesame!', and says: 'The cupboard and the chest of drawers are *things, which may be opened*'.[28] They are therefore connected with the basic actions of hiding and revealing, of conserving and remembering.

The interaction of levels

The levels of existential space form a structured totality which corresponds to the structure of existence. Man exists in relation to many objects: to physical objects, psychic objects, social objects and cultural objects.[29] *All* these objects he encounters at several levels: the levels of things, of house, of city and of landscape. And yet there still seems to be a natural correspondence between objects and levels. Did not man always search for God in nature?[30] Did he not meet his fellow men in the city, and did he not find himself

in the house? Did not the things give him the physical assurance of grasping and holding? From the level of things to the level of nature the range widens at the same time as precision decreases. In things everything is *focused*, in nature everything is *contained*. And in between there is man's dwelling. From his dwelling he can search out as well as he can look in; he can find the depth of distance as well as the depth of nearness. The levels of thing, of dwelling and of nature, therefore, are general properties of existential space, but they do not always appear in the same way. We have already mentioned variation in the public and private aspects of dwelling, and hinted at the fact that modern man to a large extent has lost the level of nature. The easiest level to preserve through all changes seems to be the level of things. But is it really preserved today, when everything is thrown away after use?

It is of great importance that the levels can *represent* each other, which is also a consequence of the fact that 'things focus' and 'nature contains'.[31] On the one hand, things, houses and cities may be cosmological symbols, or a house or a thing may represent a city etc., or again the cosmological image may imitate the form of a city, a house or a thing. Such representations probably result from the common tendency to imagine things unknown on the model of things known, or from practical difficulties in realizing a certain image on the appropriate level. A representation from the top towards the bottom of the hierarchy means that the higher levels are 'concretized' by the lower. In other words, man 'receives' the environment and makes it focus in concrete buildings and things. The things thereby 'articulate' the environment and make its character precise. That is the basic function of *detail* in our surroundings. The details 'explain' the environmental character, and thereby become meaningful. Even the *genius loci*, therefore, needs man's concretization and, in fact, is mainly known through such a manifest influence. A representation from the bottom towards the top means that man 'projects' himself into the environment. He communicates something to the environment, which in turn unifies his 'things' in a larger meaningful context. The interaction between man and the environment, therefore, consists of two complementary processes which are directed inwards and outwards respectively, in accordance with Piaget's principle of assimilation and accommodation. The level-hierarchy of existential space is therefore a product of man's taking possession of his environment.

Existential space can also be described as a simultaneous totality where the levels interact to form a complex, dynamic *field*. Through perception, parts of the field are experienced, but the general image exists independently of the individual situation. This field is neither continuous nor uniform.

Firstly it contains a system of centres, with one centre usually dominating. The centres can be inside each other, as when we think of the different 'known' places of a town, which as a whole functions as a centre in a larger context, or when we think of the various places or foci of a house. This means that the levels contain each other. On each level, the centres are related by paths. It follows that domains may also contain subdomains as well as places and paths. The degree of acquaintance with an area, therefore, is determined by the sub-elements known. These elements, on the other hand, are influenced by the character of the surrounding domain. In general, we may say that existential space consists of several overlapping and inter-penetrating systems which interact with each other.[32] In such a complex totality ambiguity and conflicts are bound to occur, it is even maintained that they ought to occur, because of 'the richness and ambiguity of (modern) experience'.[33] The question of complexity has been discussed by Amos Rapoport and Robert E. Kantor who refer to recent works by psychologists investigating the degree of environmental complexity preferred.[34] In general, human beings prefer complex environments to simple ones. Experiments with rats have shown that an enriched environment produces an increase in brain weight and intellectual capacity. 'Since healthy behaviour is exploratory, varying, venturesome in nature, it requires an environment which allows, indeed encourages, the development and exercise of such behaviour . . . Yet this preference for the complex and ambiguous is not limitless. Stimuli which are too simple lead to quick boredom; those which are too complex lead to confusion and avoidance. This suggests the idea that for each person there is an optimal perceptual rate.'[35] The authors also discuss a similar interest in ambiguity among present-day architects and quote Aldo van Eyck who says: 'Each place is multi-suggestive.' In particular van Eyck gives importance to the inside-outside relation. His statements reflect what we have found to be basic properties of existential space, and van Eyck himself realizes the determining force behind it, when he says: 'Man is both centre bound and horizon bound'.[36] The structure of existential space expresses the incessant tensions inherent in life.

32 The *island* represents a relatively closed system and may therefore give rise to a particular kind of existential space. We may also point out the common root in the words 'island' and 'isolate'. See Lynch *The Image of the City* p. 129

33 R. Venturi *Complexity and Contradiction in Architecture* New York 1966, p. 22

34 A. Rapoport and R. E. Kantor 'Complexity and Ambiguity in Environmental Design' *American Institute of Planners Journal*, July 1967

35 A. Rapoport and R. E. Kantor 'Complexity and Ambiguity in Environmental Design' p. 214

36 A. Rapoport and R. E. Kantor 'Complexity and Ambiguity in Environmental Design' p. 216

37 M. Heidegger *Sein und Zeit*, p. 104

38 K. Lynch *The Image of the City* 1960, p. 128

39 See Bollnow *Mensch und Raum* 1963, p. 212 who quotes the poem by Hermann Hesse
Seltsam, im Nebel zu wandern!
Einsam ist jeder Busch und Stein,
kein Baum sieht den andern, jeder ist allein . . .
Seltsam, im Nebel zu wandern!
Leben ist Einsamsein.
Kein Mensch kennt den andern,
jeder ist allein.
(it is strange to walk in fog when every bush and stone stands solitary, no tree sees the other, each is alone . . . It is strange to walk in fog. Life is being solitary. No man knows another, each is alone) Bollnow *op. cit.* p. 220

39a (dusk falls from above, soon all proximity is far)

40 H. Sedlmayr 'Ursprung und Anfänge der Kunst' *Epochen und Werke* I, 1959, p. 9

41 O. F. Bollnow *Mensch und Raum* 1963, pp. 257ff

42 O.F. Bollnow *Mensch und Raum* 1963, p. 264

Conclusion

It has been maintained that the development of an existential space forms a necessary part of the orientation of the individual, and that the basic properties of its structure ought to be public, in order to allow for social integration. Orientation and social integration, however, have many dimensions. Space is only one of the aspects of existence. Could not, for instance, social integration be achieved by cultural or political means rather than by the development of common space concepts? We do not want to reduce the importance of any of the dimensions of human action, but should point out that *any* activity has spatial aspects, because any activity implies movements and relations to places. Existence and existential space cannot be separated. Heidegger says:'The world at any time reveals the spatiality of the space which belongs to it.'[37] Any activity means 'to be somewhere'.

What, then, does it mean 'to be somewhere'? It simply means to be located in one's existential space. We may be 'at home', 'away' or 'astray'. The term 'away' expresses that we are on our way to get 'somewhere else'. The German word *weg*, in fact, means 'way' as well as 'away'. The term 'lost' expresses that we have left the known structure of existential space. The *experience* (perception) of space, thus, consists in the tension between one's immediate situation and existential space. When our immediate location coincides with the centre of our existential space, we experience being 'at home'. If not, we are either 'on our way', 'somewhere else', or we are 'lost'.

'To be somewhere', however, has many forms. Bollnow talks about 'Der Handlungsraum' (space of action), 'Der gestimmte Raum' (expressive space) and 'Der Raum des menschlichen Zusammenlebens' (space of human interaction). The space of action may also be called 'space of work', and consists mainly in a spatial organization of objects for use.[38] Expressive space, on the other hand, is determined by affective identification. Bollnow refers to the varying character of natural space, and talks at length about the forest, which is generally experienced as being simultaneously closed and open. This character furthermore changes with day and night and with the climatic conditions. As particularly interesting phenomena, Bollnow mentions the effect of snow and of fog,[39] and of dawn and dusk. He quotes the well known verse by Goethe:

'Dämmrung senkte sich von oben,
schon ist alle Nähe fern . . .'.[39a]

The concepts of 'narrow' and 'wide' are especially suitable for describing such 'character'. 'Narrow' is what restricts life (but in certain cases: protects life), while 'wide' is what allows life to unfold. The expression or character of the environment, therefore, is neither something subjective within man, nor something to be found outside, but an aspect of man's being in the world. The expressive spaces created by man primarily aim at the realization of such characters. In fact, Sedlmayr defines art as the 'shaping of an intelligible character' and says, 'the achievement of the artist lies in creating an intelligible equivalent for the particular complex that he has experienced'.[40]

In the space of human interaction, the spaces of action and of expression are unified to create, in its highest form, what Bollnow calls 'the space of loving communal life'.[41] He points out that marriage among primitive people is often connected with the building of a house and says: 'The space which they (the lovers) jointly produce is their home.'[42] When space of love becomes public, as a common ideal image of existential space, it gains the character of a *sacred* space. Sacred space always centres on one or more sacred places, that is, *foci* where the common cosmic image is represented. Often the centres are connected by sacred paths which lead to the meaningful goal. Pilgrimage, thus, is one of the great symbols of human existence.[43]

The sacred path implies that 'to be on the way' also has many forms. It is closely related to the problem of pace and rhythm, that is, the changing character of movement. In fact, *how* we get from one place to another is a basic aspect of man's being in the world. We can run, stroll, march or dance, thereby expressing different ways of taking possession of the environment. Life itself can be understood as a movement from one condition to another. This movement is incessant and continuous, but it has rhythm and form. Even man's basic organic needs, such as hunger and thirst, follow rhythmic patterns. Furthermore, man is part of a system of natural rhythms, such as night and day, the change of seasons and his own 'ages'. Piaget says appropriately: 'Life is a creator of patterns'.[44] In other words, we become what we do. In this sense, life interprets itself as space by taking possession of the environment.

To conclude we may say a few words about some actual problems connected with man's existential space. Whereas the human environment so far has had a structure corresponding to the existential space described above, present-day development seems to favour a new *mobility*. Technical means of communication have freed us from direct human contact, and an increasing number of people have become physically mobile. Many seem to believe that this development offers possibilities for a richer social interaction. Thus the American city-planning theorist Melvin Webber says: 'It is interaction, not place, that is the essence of the city and city life'.[45] The Dutch utopist Constant Nieuwenhuis has given a particularly illuminating image of a mobile world in his 'New Babylon' fantasy. He says: 'In New Babylon people would be constantly travelling. There would be no need for them to return to their point of departure as this in any case would be transformed . . . It follows that New Babylon

could not have a determined plan. On the contrary, every element would be left undetermined, mobile and flexible.'[46] But such a mobile world, which is not based on the repetition of similarities in connection with a stable system of places, would make human development impossible. Piaget's research indicates that a mobile world would tie man to an 'egocentric' stage, while a stable and structured world frees his intelligence. Nor would a mobile world allow for real human interaction. Christopher Alexander thus points out that 'the social pathologies associated with urban life – deliquency and mental disorder – follow inevitably from the lack of intimate contact'. To have such an intimate contact 'the people concerned must see each other very often, almost every day'. He also maintains that mental disturbances occur when people only have 'nonpatterned encounters with each other'.[47] In fact, it is a misunderstanding to believe that a stable world and corresponding environmental images hamper man's mobility. Kevin Lynch says that 'the environmental image has its original function in permitting purposeful mobility', and 'the terror of being lost comes from the necessity that a mobile organism be oriented in its surroundings'.[48] Heidegger furthermore points out 'When I go towards the exit of a room I am already there and would not be able to go there unless I was already there.'[49] In other words, *mobility* presupposes a structured image of the environment, an existential space which contains generalized as well as particular orientations.

The discussion of the human environment has thus taken a new direction. Until a few years ago we discussed whether man ought to live in one-family houses or flats. Today we have penetrated deeper into the problem and ask what we should demand in order to make the environment a satisfactory part of human existence. As an answer to this question, the idea of a mobile world is anything but realistic. It confuses psychic and physical mobility, as well as psychic and physical distance, and substitutes real identification with a chaotic consumption of stimuli. Hans Sedlmayr has grasped the tendency at its very root, talking about 'the lost centre'.[50] The environmental

43 See K. Goldammer *Die Formenwelt des Religiösen* 1960, ch. IV, 2 'Heiliger Raum und heiliger Weg'

44 J. Piaget *The Psychology of Intelligence* 1950, p. 167

45 M. M. Webber 'Urban Place and Nonplace Urban Realm' *Explorations into Urban Structure* 1964

46 C. Nieuwenhuis 'New Babylon' *Architectural Design* June 1964

47 C. Alexander 'The City as a Mechanism for sustaining Human Contact' *Environment for Man* ed. W. R. Ewald 1967.

48 K. Lynch *The Image of the City* 1960, pp. 124, 125

49 M. Heidegger 'Bauen Wohnen Denken' p. 32

50 H. Sedlmayr *Art in Crisis : the lost centre* 1957

51 M. Heidegger 'Bauen Wohnen Denken' 1954 p. 23

52 R. Schwarz *Von der Bebauung der Erde* 1949, p. 12

problem we are facing, therefore, is not of a technical, economical, social or political nature. It is a human problem, the problem of preserving man's identity. In his 'free' arrogance he departed from his place and 'conquered' the world. But he is left with emptiness and no real freedom. He has forgotten what it means to 'dwell', and remember Rilke's words:

'O Heimweh der Stätten, die nicht genug Geliebt wurden, einst in flüchtigen
                                                    Stunden –
Wie gern gäb ich ihnen, handelnd von Fern Versäumtes, den Umriss abzurunden.'

The Odyssey is still a valid tale.

Perhaps man's departure was motivated by a wrong idea of 'freedom'. Heidegger reminds us that the words 'dwell', 'protection', 'peace' and 'freedom' originally belonged together,[51] and everything seems to indicate that this is still the case. Freedom still presupposes security, and security is only possible through the human identity of which existential space is one aspect. This is the essence of 'dwelling'. But we have to learn to dwell. In fact, our experience today shows us that man does not spontaneously find his foothold. The problem of environment, therefore, is a problem of intentions and attitudes. As Rudolf Schwarz says: 'Man cannot plan the world without designing himself.'[52]

3 Architectural space

It is the city which should be judged though we, its children, must pay the price.

Lawrence Durrell *Justine*.

The elements of architectural space

Architectural space may be defined as a 'concretization' of existential space. 'Existential space' is a psychological concept, denoting the schemata man develops, interacting with the environment, in order to get along satisfactorily. The result of this interaction, however, will not be a finished, complete image, it will normally contain contradictions, and parts will be missing, for example, the feeling of belonging to a particular place. When a group of 'lost' young people in Oslo recently protested against the commercialized use of land and buildings in the centre of the city, their slogan was: 'a place to stay'. The environmental image, therefore, comprises wishes and dreams. To satisfy these wishes, man tries to *change* his environment. In other words, architecture concretizes an image which goes beyond the already existing environment. It always reflects a wish to *improve* man's conditions. Man's existential space is thus determined by the concrete structure of the environment, but his needs and wishes create a feedback. The relationship between man and environment is therefore a two-way process, a real interaction. 'Architectural space' is a concrete, physical aspect of this process.[1] We could also say that existential space, being one of the psychic structures which form part of man's being in the world, has architectural space as its physical counterpart.[2]

Ideally, there should be an isomorphic relation between existential and architectural space but, in practice, this is not fully achieved. Architectural space is given 'ready made' to the individual, that is, it is the creation of others and reflects *their* existential spaces. A particular attitude is therefore needed to grasp its structure,[3] and when we try to create architectural spaces which concretize our existential space, the result may not be liked by others. Man's relation to architectural space therefore consists, on the one hand, in trying to integrate its structure into his personal schemata, and on the other in translating his schemata into concrete architectural structures. In order that he succeed in the first, and that the second may become a contribution to the development of the existential spaces of others, architectural space must necessarily have a pronounced *public* character. To understand this better, we may introduce a simple model which represents three 'levels of generalization'; the private or individual, the public or social and the objective or scientific.

Our private world is obviously based on a series of generalizations, as we order our experiences according to their similarities. But the concepts or 'objects' we arrive at have relatively imprecise boundaries and a low degree of articulation. Our conception

1 To simplify the problem we do not here distinguish between 'natural' and man-made elements in the environment. What man *selects* from nature to serve his purposes, we also call 'architecture'

2 This does not mean, however, that we reduce architecture to its physical aspects. Architectural space represents existential space, and thereby the 'higher' social and cultural objects of man's world

3 Hans Sedlmayr was the first to stress that the work of art requires an 'adequate attitude' from the perceiver. See 'Zu einer strengen Kunstwissenschaft' *Kunstwissenschaftliche Forschungen* 1, 1931

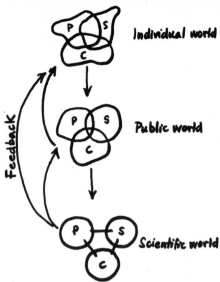

Individual world

Feedback

Public world

Scientific world

4 Interference leads to what Egon Brunswik has called 'intermediary objects'. The phenomena perceived are intermediary objects, while science aims at the abstraction of 'pure' objects. See Norberg-Schulz *Intentions in Architecture* 1963, pp. 32ff

5 See C. Norberg-Schulz 'Meaning in Architecture' *Meaning in Architecture* ed. C. Jencks and G. Baird 1969

6 See C. Norberg-Schulz *Intentions in Architecture* 1963, p. 31

generalized structure than the individual, but is obviously deprived of all the varying shades which distinguish the latter. As a matter of course, the public world has, to a greater extent than the individual, to make use of scientific insight. It is therefore more objective, but may never *correspond* to the *scientific world*, which is characterized by the disappearance of interference, as far as that is possible, or, in other words, by the absence of values. Only by leaving out values does science become 'exact'. The scientific world is a world of precisely defined and lawfully interrelated objects. As it is interference which determines what we call 'qualities', it is natural to characterize the scientific world as 'quantitative'. If the public world corresponded to the scientific all meaningful feelings and expressive activities would become impossible.

One of the key words used above is 'value'. To possess a system of values means that one wants and is convinced that the world *ought to have* a certain structure. Values, therefore, influence our choice of alternatives, they make our actions *intentional*. They may even lead us to accept solutions which are disadvantageous from a practical point of view. Such solutions can be defended if they are necessary to manifest values needed by society. They should, however, be rejected if they only express private idiosyncrasies. When we lay stress on the word *intention*, it is to say that both the (environmental) needs and the (architectural) forms which satisfy them are the result of meaningful choices (conscious or unconscious). This holds both for perception and production. Only in exceptional circumstances do we intend forms which correspond exactly to the measurable, physical stimulus. Usually the stimulus symbolizes a 'higher' objective, that is, we experience a meaning.[5] We thus *interpret* the situation *relative* to a system of values. To avoid becoming a victim of prejudice, it is essential that perception be based on a value system which gives the stimulus an *adequate* meaning, that is, a sufficient 'intentional depth'.[6] A modern pluralistic society where different value systems interfere, makes great demands on the intentional depth. We therefore ought to have knowledge of value systems other than

of a tree, for instance, may only consist in a general idea of its shape or colour. A gardener or a botanist, however, will probably have a more complete conception. This is because individual worlds (within a particular field) have been further structured by special knowledge, which in our diagram is illustrated by a feedback-arrow from science. But man's individual concepts are not only vague, they also have an inevitable tendency to *interfere*. A man's concept of a tree is thus influenced by the situation in which it is experienced: harvesting apples, climbing the branches, or engraving a heart pierced by an arrow. In fact, it is this interference[4] which gives things individual 'colour' and makes the individual world something more than a mechanical reaction to physical stimuli. But at the same time is is clear that this interference, if it took place in an accidental and subjective way, would have catastrophic consequences for our intercourse with physical things as well as with other people. Individual concepts and interference patterns must, therefore, be based on *social* experiences. This is also illustrated in the diagram by a feedback-arrow. In other words, our different individual worlds must have common basic structural properties to enable us to become part of society. These common concepts and interference patterns we may call the *public world*. The public world is characterized by a more stable and the one we personally profess, and be able to change attitudes when necessary. But the different systems ought also to have some basic properties in common to avoid inherent conflicts in society. When we say that forms are 'expressive', it therefore means that they manifest higher objectives, which eventually are based on systems of values. The forms are expressive because they engage, because they mean something to us. We could also talk about 'symbolic forms', whereby 'symbol' means something quite different from a naïve depiction. 'Expressive forms' and 'symbolic forms' are, therefore, synonyms, signifying that measurable physical forms (perceived or produced) mediate a higher meaning. The symbol-function is basic to all human behaviour. Without symbols which concretize his value-oriented being in the world, man would be inexpressive.

How, then, does architecture enter this model? Should the environment we create be adapted to the private, the public or the scientific world? It is obvious that the last alternative has to be rejected. It is of course possible to reduce architecture to a mere rationalistic activity, and hope that the other arts succeed in showing man that his world is meaningful. Our analysis of existential space, however, tells us that this reduction would make man 'homeless' in the widest sense of the term. Let us therefore hope that our environment may still acquire a 'meaning' to transcend the merely practical aspect. Should it, in this case, correspond to the private or the public world? As it is one of the purposes of architecture to help integrate the individual in a common form, the first alternative is not satisfactory. That is, individual needs certainly have to be satisfied, but they have to be understood, as part of a larger context. In other words, even our individual expressions ought to have a common denominator. In general, architecture should serve the *public* world. This does not mean that we hypothesize *one* collective system of values and let everything be determined by that; rather we should use the *role-structure* of society as our basis; a problem, however, that we have discussed in further detail in other contexts.[7]

In conclusion, architectural space concretizes a public existential space which includes many private existential spaces. It is a symbolic form which mediates the higher objects of man's world through a certain structural similarity, whereby the places, paths, domains and levels of existential space find their concrete, physical counterpart – a fact which follows logically from the discussion of existential space. Creating architectural space, therefore, means integrating an intended form of life in the environment. Rudolf Schwarz says: 'People put the earth within them in the land they find, place the landscape within them on the landscape without, and both become one.'[8]

Place and node

The first problem to discuss is the architectural definition of 'centre'. It has already been shown that centre means the creation of a place, or, in Lynch's terminology a 'node'. Lynch says: 'Nodes are the strategic foci into which the observer can enter, typically either junctions of paths, or concentrations of some characteristic'.[9] Lynch also introduces the term 'landmark' to denote 'point references considered to be external to the observer'.[10] Landmarks often correspond to centres in existential space, but sometimes their function is more to indicate boundaries or directions. In general, the definition of a place is based on the Gestalt principles of proximity and closure. Proximity creates a clustering of elements, that is, a concentration of masses. Hence we find throughout the history of architecture the tendency to mark a place by means of a large mass. Enclosure, on the other hand, determines a space which is separated from its surroundings as a particular place. Such spaces exist in nature, for instance as caves. The initiation rites of the Dogons take place in caves, and the centre of meaning is furthermore indicated by a concentrated mass placed inside the cave, an erect stone of phallic character.[11] We thus find the two original architectural symbols of place brought together.

D. Frey discusses the 'mass-centre' or *Mal-Motiv* extensively. He points out that the mass expresses the condition of *being*

7 See C. Norberg-Schulz 'Intention und Methode in der Architektur' *Der Architekt* 6/1967

8 R. Schwarz *Von der Bebauung der Erde* 1949, p. 59

9 K. Lynch *The Image of the City* 1960, p. 72

10 K. Lynch *The Image of the City* 1960, p. 78

11 See H. Haan 'Dogon' *Byggekunst* 2/1965 p. 32

12   D. Frey *Grundlegung zu einer vergleichenden Kunstwissenschaft*, pp. 6, 58

somewhere, in contrast to the movement to and from, and that space is centralized by the erection of such a *Mal*.

'The motif of the standing figure bears the same relationship to sculptural representation of the body as the Mal (goal) to the shaping of architectural space. In this stationary centre or goal the very space is systematized as a stationary shape.'[12]

In the Egyptian pyramid we find the strongest expression of absolute existence; it is not a place for human activities in the normal sense of the word, but the goal for the path of life. Tombs, in fact, generally have a centralized form. The ability of a mass to serve as a 'centre', could be described by the term 'concentration'. Concentration is a function of the main shape, as

(3) *Acropolis* Athens, fifth century BC

well as the treatment of details. In general it is strengthened by a continuous bounding surface and by symmetry. The sphere, hence, has a maximum of concentration.[13] Concentration is also enhanced by isolation: when a mass is lifted up in relation to its surroundings, a vertical axis is implied, around which space is organized. The isolation of the Acropolis in Athens from the profane domain around not only enhances its sacredness but makes it an organizing centre for the whole local world. Mediaeval towns in Europe usually get their strong place character from a combination of

13 For a more extensive discussion of the properties of mass elements see C. Norberg-Schulz *Intentions in Architecture* 1963, pp. 134ff

(4) *Town Square* with town-hall (1559) and Jesuit church (1656 **D. Orsini**), Klatovy, Bohemia

clustering and vertical accents. In the town of Klatovy a most impressive 'double focus' is created by the towers of the town hall and the church. In general, the mass is a symbolic or ideal centre, rather than a real place of activity. It puts a stop to the horizontal extension of man's environment, and makes his need for fixed points visible.

The place of activity has roots which are just as old as those of the concentrated mass. The enclosure, in fact, may be considered man's first real attempt to take possession of the environment.

(5) **Kjell Lund** and **Nils Slaatto** *St Halvard's Church*, Oslo 1966

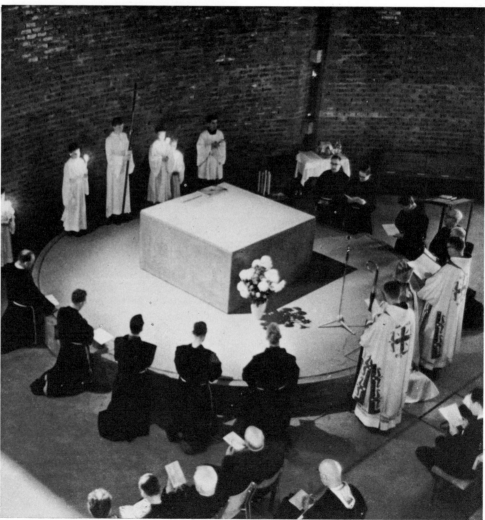

'Man's first architecturally important intrusion into his environment – dominated by magical forces – was the definition and enclosure of a domain, the temenos, and by this very act of definition the domain obtained a special relationship to these forces. Here they should dwell or be kept out. This domain fixed the emotionally insecure limits between the ego and the outer world.'[14]

14 G. Bandmann *Mittelalterliche Architektur als Bedeutungsträger* 1951, pp. 133ff

° (6) *Roman amphitheatre* Nîmes, Augustan period

(7) *Wasserburg am Inn* Bavaria

(8) **Sinan** *his own tomb*
Istanbul 1588

(8) **Sinan** *his own tomb*
Istanbul 1588

Whereas the mass-centre has an abstract, ideal character, the enclosure has strong social implications. Basically it expresses a coming together, the forming of a ring for a common purpose. Most cultures have such enclosures where rituals or theatrical performances take place. The essential architectural property is a clearly defined boundary, which secures physical as well as psychic protection. In the Roman amphitheatre the effect of enclosure is enhanced by the geometrized form (which however contains directions) and by the rows of seats falling down towards the middle. The regular

(9) **Bernardo A. Vittone**
Capella della Visitazione,
Vallinotto 1738

(10) **Bernardo A. Vittone**
Capella della Visitazione,
Vallinotto: interior

distribution of openings also expresses the role of the building as a 'social' centre. While the enclosed single space forms a complement to the concentrated mass, the enclosed settlement corresponds to the cluster of closely spaced elements. The boundaries of such settlements may be natural or artificial, but in both cases a clear distinction between inside and outside is essential to the character of place. In many cases we find denseness as well as enclosure, whereby a still stronger identity is achieved. We will, however, return to the question of defining types of places when discussing the various environmental levels.

The mass-centre and the enclosure both represent an 'either-or'. Only fairly late during the course of architectural history were buildings created which realized in equal measure both aspects of the place concept. This development was closely tied to the building of Christian churches and achieved its most convincing results with the great domed structures of the Renaissance period. About the same time Sinan carried through related intentions in the large mosques of Istanbul.[15] The centralized spaces thereby created, were varied *ad infinitum*, but basically they always represent what Schwarz calls a 'sacred ring', 'One of

15 The centralized mosque, however, always contains a 'difficult' contradiction, as it is directed towards Mecca

45

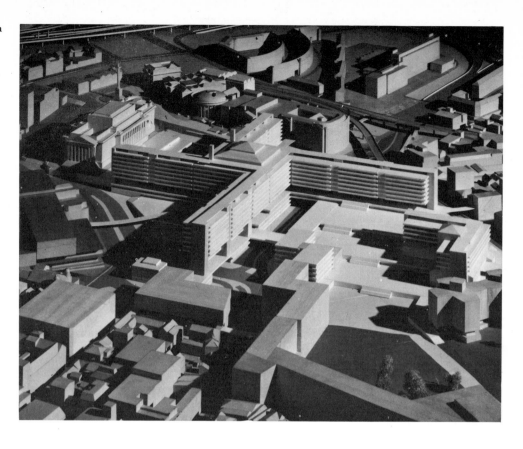

(11) **Colin St John Wilson**
Civic Centre Liverpool,
begun in 1966

16 R. Schwarz
The Church Incarnate 1958,
p. 29

the strong figures that builds the world'.[16]
In the eighteenth century Bernardo Vittone
still varied the double theme of the centralized place in a series of perfect buildings.
Even in modern architecture the great
centralized hall appears as an urban focus.
Particularly convincing is the solution of
Colin St John Wilson for the new Civic
Centre at Liverpool, where four adminis-
tration buildings branch out from a vertically
directed space which is lit from above. This
project clearly demonstrates the fundamental
and timeless character of man's need for a
'centre'.

A place, however, not only becomes a
centre because it functions as a goal in existential space. We have seen that it is just as
important to regard it as a 'point of departure'. The tension between centripetal and
centrifugal forces, therefore, constitutes the
essence of any place. Michelangelo must have

(12) **Colin St John Wilson**
Civic Centre : interior

(13) **Le Corbusier**
La Tourette Eveux, near
Lyons 1952–60

17 Michelangelo's intentions were partly changed by della Porta and others, who stressed the longitudinal axis changing several important details

felt this when he created his Capitoline Square in Rome. His composition essentially consists of two elements: an oval inscribed in the floor of the *piazza* by means of two descending steps, and three buildings which form a circumscribed trapezium. The oval is clearly characterized as expanding, as it is decorated by a star-like pattern which increases in scale towards the periphery. Furthermore the oval is convex and 'breaks through' the surrounding surface. The trapezium, however, seems to contract, as the two lateral buildings converge towards the open side of the piazza. In the original project all three buildings were articulated in a similar way, creating a continuous boundary.[17] The project has been interpreted as expressing the idea of the Capitoline Hill as the *caput mundi*. The oval, thus, would be nothing less than the very top of our globe. This interpretation is supported by the fact that Michelangelo here succeeded in symbolizing the essence of place, as perhaps nobody else in the history of architecture. The conflict between the expanding oval with the statue of the Emperor (i.e. man)

48

in the centre, and the contracting boundary, in fact contains the basic problem of existential space, giving it a 'tragic' note. Few people escape the fascination of the Capitoline Square, which touches the deepest ground of our psyche.

The place as a synthesis of arrival and departure and of inside and outside, is symbolized in a still more direct and less tragic way in some of the great works of the Baroque period. As a particularly convincing and charming example we may mention the small chapel of St John Nepomuk in Göllersdorf by Hildebrandt. Here a centralized baldacchino defines and keeps a place in the most fundamental manner. An opening in the crowning dome stresses the vertical axis, and the diagonally directed columns add a note of dynamic expansion. The little structure is thus both a centre of attention and of 'radiation', and satisfies the basic existential demands on the centre.[18]

In all the examples mentioned above, the place is defined by means of certain topological properties. We ought also to mention, however, that some places are defined simply by being strongly dissimilar to their surroundings. This may hold true for 'natural' places as well as man-made settlements. Sometimes such a particular character is combined with a strong topological definition to create what Lynch has called 'a distinct and unforgettable place'.

Path and axis

Kevin Lynch defines paths as 'the channels along which the observer customarily, occasionally, or potentially moves'.[19] We could also add 'ideally' moves. The organizing axis, in fact, is not intended for real movement, but represents a symbolic direction which unifies a number of elements among themselves, and often relates them to a larger totality. Often, however, path and axis are identical. The real path and the more abstract axis may both have horizontal as well as vertical components. In general,

18 R. Schwarz *The Church Incarnate* 1958

19 K. Lynch *The Image of the City* 1960, p. 47

(16) *Temple of Queen Hatshepsut* Thebes, Egypt 1400 BC (XVIII dynasty)

(17) *Temple of Fortuna*
Praeneste (Palestrina) first
century BC

(18) Drawing of *Temple
of Fortuna*

20 D. Frey *Grundlegung
zu einer vergleichenden
Kunstwissenschaft,* p. 82

21 H. Kähler 'Das
Fortunaheiligtum von
Palestrina Praeneste'
*Annales Universitatis
Saraviensis* vol. VII, Fasc.
3, 4. 1958, p. 218

the definition of a path or an axis is based on
the Gestalt principle of continuity, and on a
certain similarity of the mass or space
elements taking part in the 'composition'.
Settlements organized as a linear succession
of units are found in folk architecture from
all parts of the world, and are usually
determined by geographical factors, as well
as particular types of work and communication. In ancient Egypt, however, the path
became a dominant symbolic form. The
tomb-temples of the Ancient Kingdom are
architectural paths consisting of long corri-
dors leading from the reception building on
the Nile to the main temple at the foot of
the pyramid. In the temple of Queen
Hatshepsut near Deir-el-Bahari, the theme
is made still more explicit, as the path has
become an axis which divides the building
into two symmetrical parts. The mountain
itself takes over the role of the pyramid.
'It is the most magnificent and consistent
attempt to do away with the incessant
passage of time as part of human fate by
means of an architectural structure.'[20]

Whereas the Egyptian temples are based on
one straight path leading 'in' towards a
final but unreachable goal, the larger Roman
layouts show a complex system of movements. In the Republican sanctuary of
Fortuna at Praeneste (Palestrina) we are
already finding a characteristic doubling of
the paths on both sides of the main axis,
while only part of the axis is used for real
movement. Thus the perceiver takes possession of the total environment, and when he
looks back from the fourth terrace, he almost
has the feeling of flying like a bird over the
plain below, towards the distant sea at Anzio.
The whole landscape becomes part of the
architectural solution, and is formed by
means of terraces, porches, stairs, ramps and
fountains. The main direction is not inwards
but upwards. 'This upward movement is
a force in the structured space and is combined with a great freedom that reveals itself
in the relation between the layout, its parts
and the surrounding landscape.'[21] The
existential space symbolized here is different
from the Egyptian. It is a space which is
expansive and open to the world; it does
not only express the success of its builder
Sulla, but the general attitude of the Roman

people. Other characteristic path structures can also be found in antiquity. The architecture of the ancient Orient, for instance, is based on circulating movements, which reinforce the dominating wish for static places, rather than forming real paths.

The character of a path is thus determined by its relation to places. It either leads towards a goal, away from a point of departure, or it forms a ring around the place, expressing that 'existence is round'. As any place lives from the tension between centripetal and centrifugal forces, place and path must be interdependent.

In the early Christian church the interior space is a 'place' apart and different from the world outside, but it is interpreted as a path. Like a colonnaded Roman street the nave leads towards the altar in the apse, expressing that the path is the essence of existence. The path of the Christian church, however, is not without hope, like that of the Egyptian temple; it has a beginning and an end. The end is represented by the altar, which tells us that the path of life has found, and continues to find, its end in Jesus Christ. 'People become part of a history that they

51

Architectural history offers many examples which illustrate the concretization of more particular path structures. In garden architecture, for instance, the path has always been an important element, unifying different domains. A charming solution to this problem of unification is found in Villa Lante near Viterbo. Contrary to later Baroque solutions, the building does not function as the focus and goal of the composition. It has, in fact, been split into two small casinos which, symmetrically placed on both sides of the main axis, only play an accompanying role. This axis is a path, but not a path for walking along. Rather it is the path of a small brook which starts in a grotto at a point where the villa approaches free nature. After many adventures the course of water ends in an artificial 'lake' down at the *parterre*. This 'path' is obviously an allegory of nature, with man taking part by means of architecture, sculpture and painting. In the Baroque parks the taking possession of nature by means of paths culminates. The motive of the star radiating out from a

(22) **Jacapo Barozzi Vignola** *Villa Lante*
Bagnaia, near Viterbo,
begun in 1566

must live through again and yet which has already come to an end, and in that end overcame death and found salvation.'[22] The theme of the sacred path found its most splendid interpretation in the Gothic churches. The continuity in depth was no longer expressed simply by lateral columns or pillars, but by the interpenetrating ribs of the vaulting, whose complex movement searches constantly for a place to rest.

The horizontal integration which determines movement in depth, also characterizes old streets of historical towns. While the church represents an ideal movement, and therefore shows a geometrical structure, the street is a real path serving the physical and social actions of man, which are better interpreted in terms of topological relations. We will, however, return to the analysis of street structure when discussing the urban level.

22 R. Schwarz *The Church Incarnate*, p. 102

(23) **J. C. Schlaun**
*Project for Schloss
Clemenswerth* near Soegel,
Niedersachsen 1736

centre was developed by French architects during the seventeenth century, and came to dominate man's environment. A map of Paris and its environs from 1740 shows a system of centres and radiating roads which transform the world into a network of paths, expressing a new existential feeling of openness and expansion.[23] A late, but particularly clear example of this intention is found in Schlaun's project for Clemenswerth. While the Baroque network really joins different foci, the modern network of motorways is a mere infrastructure, never leading to any goal but passing by everything.

We have already mentioned the bridge as a particular kind of path. A river may be said to separate and unify simultaneously. It divides the land, but also defines a space which is common to both shores. The unifying effect is usually strengthened by the land sloping down towards the water, and by the river serving as a means of communication. The bridge makes it possible for man to take possession of the 'river-space'. Here he feels

23 See E. N. Bacon *Design of Cities* 1957, pp. 180–181

53

outside and inside, free and protected at the same time, moving back and forth between two domains which are different, although belonging to the same totality. These tensions are beautifully expressed by the Charles Bridge in Prague (1353). Built on the remains of an older structure, it has a most unusual curved course which is experienced as a continuation of the narrow and crooked streets on both sides. The Charles Bridge is 'populated' by statues which make it a real civic centre. Other paths of a different kind

(24) *Charles Bridge*
Prague 1353 (with statues from the eighteenth century)

(25) *Charles Bridge*

are the staircase and the urban flight of stairs. Built to conquer a difference of levels, they are basically vertical. Giving the feeling of victory over gravity, they have a strong expressive content. An unusual fascination has always been exercised by spiral stair-cases, where one really experiences rising up along the vertical axis. Urban stairs have often served as the link between a sanctuary at the top and a crowded piazza at the bottom, thereby concretizing the transition from one existential level to another. In the

(26) **Jacapo Barozzi Vignola** *Farnese Palace* Caprarola: spiral staircase 1558–73

(27) **Francesco de Sanctis**
Spanish Steps Rome 1723–25

Spanish Steps in Rome we also find a subtle tension between the axis and the pulsating movement of the two symmetrical flights of steps.

The examples mentioned above show that continuity in depth may be created by articulating the floor, the walls, or the ceiling, or any of these elements in combination. Continuity as such is independent of geometry. Rather it is determined by 'guiding elements' which simultaneously belong to two or more superior elements (buildings, spaces).[24]

Domain and district

Kevin Lynch defines districts as areas 'which the observer can mentally go inside of, and which are recognizable as having some common, identifying character'.[25] 'The physical characteristics that determine districts are thematic continuities which may consist of an endless variety of components: texture,

24 See C. Norberg-Schulz *Intentions in Architecture* 1963, p. 143

25 K. Lynch *The Image of the City* 1960, p. 47

(28) **Le Corbusier**
Carpenter Art Centre
Harvard University,
Cambridge, Mass.

space, form, detail, symbol, building type, use, activity, inhabitants, topography.' Together such properties lead to the formation of a 'characteristic cluster'.[26] Defined boundaries reinforce the formation of districts. In our environment we may distinguish between natural domains, mainly determined by topography and vegetation, and those formed by man as an expression of a particular activity. In both cases boundary and texture are basic defining properties, the Gestalt principles of closure and similarity. While the boundary defines a domain in relation to its surroundings,

26 K. Lynch *The Image of the City* 1960, pp. 67, 68

(29) **Eero Saarinen** *Colleges* Yale University, New Haven, Connecticut

texture gives us knowledge of the general character of the district, although we might never really have been inside. Man's need for belonging to something he knows is thereby satisfied, as the character of 'his place' is repeated throughout. On such a general textured 'ground' special domains appear as distinct 'shapes' because of a change in scale, texture, or because of the introduction of particular boundaries. The *transition* from one domain to another is a critical problem when we want to concretize a system of existential domains. The gate, therefore, was given great importance during the his-

(31) *Fishing near the Norwegian coast*

tory of architecture. We find it in nature as a straight or a pass, and on the urban level as the city gate which symbolizes the transition from nature to civilization. The history of architecture illustrates man's physical and psychic need to define his environment as consisting of domains, and the science of geography to a high extent derives its content from the same source.

Elementary interaction

In architectural space, as in existential space, place, path and domain form an integrated whole. Together they constitute what we may call a 'field'.[27] The concept of field is used in natural science to designate the spatial aspects of a system of interacting forces, and has been taken over by Kurt

27 The term *campo* has been introduced by P. Portoghesi in his book *Borromini, architettura come linguaggio* 1967, p. 384

59

28 K. Lewin *Principles of Topological Psychology* 1936

Lewin to describe man's location in a psycho-social context.[28] An 'architectural field' also consists of forces which ought to be balanced in a state of dynamic equilibrium. The field may be as simple as a single, relatively inarticulate place plus a surrounding domain, into which a few paths penetrate. Such a

(33) *Piazza dei Miracoli* Pisa, eleventh and twelfth century

(34) *Hall* near Innsbruck, Austria

limiting case hardly exists in the modern world, and already in antiquity we encounter complex fields where a number of places and domains are interrelated by means of axes and paths. In Greek architecture, however, interrelation is less important than the pronounced individuality of each element, whereas in Roman architecture a strong wish for spatial integration is evident. Hadrian's villa near Tivoli offers a characteristic example: rather than a group of single buildings, the layout consists of enclosures of varying character, which are organized by means of axes and linked by paths. The total system, however, is still additive, comprising many relatively independent sub-systems, and large areas are left over as almost blank spots on the map. During the Middle Ages European architecture hardly went beyond this stage although single buildings, such as the great cathedrals, show a high degree of spatial integration. In Renaissance architecture the idea of integration by means of repeated, simple geometrical units, resulted in principle in the establishment of a continuous field of Euclidean character. Analysing the buildings of Brunelleschi, however, we find that organizing centres play a decisive role, thus contradicting the general

(35) *Etruscan city gate* Saturnia, Tuscany

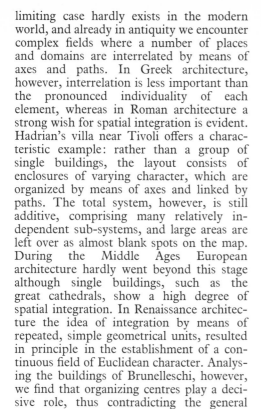

(36) *Villa Adriana* Tivoli AD 118–138 (plastic reconstruction: **I. Gismondi**)

29 See C. Norberg-Schulz
'Le ultime intenzioni di
Alberti' *Acta Institutum
Romanum Norvegiae*, vol. I,
1962

30 See C. Norberg-Schulz
Michelangelo som arkitekt
1958

(37) *St Peter's Square and
Basilica* Rome 1506–1660.
Architects: **Bramante,
Michelangelo, Maderno,
Bernini**

(38) **Leone Battista
Alberti** *S. Andrea* Mantua,
begun in 1472

Euclidean repetition. In the works of Alberti
this becomes still more evident, not only
because of a strong wish for rhythmization,
but because of the marked tension between
centralization and longitudinality. Rather
than being a problem of the church alone, it
is clear that this fundamental relation is the
determining aspect of any existential space.
No wonder, then, that those aiming to define
by their buildings man's total position in the
world, throughout the centuries returned to
centralization and longitudinality as their
main themes. In S. Andrea in Mantua the
longitudinal nave and the domed centre are
geometrically integrated,[29] but the two
aspects do not unify to form one synthetic
whole. The same, in principle, holds true
for St Peter's in Rome, in spite of Michelangelo's strong attempt at a spatial unification of the church,[30] and Bernini's creation of
a piazza which, simultaneously, has direction and is centralized. Its oval shape, in
fact, illustrates the characteristic aim of
Baroque architecture to arrive at a synthetic
solution. Up to this point architectural fields
consisted of relatively heterogeneous
elements, a state of affairs which is still

normal. In the works of Borromini, however, we encounter a new approach: all his spaces are synthetic totalities, where it is impossible to single out individual units; by inflecting the bounding surfaces he created a new continuity stretching horizontally as well as vertically. As his curved walls are determined by centres, they constitute interpenetrating centralized fields. The dynamic zones where the fields interfere are used for movement, in particular for entrances.[31] Borromini's ideas were developed further by Guarini who repeated the interrelated centres and interfering zones systematically to form extended patterns which interpret the continuous space of Renaissance architecture in dynamic terms. Guarini's fields are not based on monotonous repetition, but on *systematic* changes in density and direction.[32] It ought to be pointed out that Borromini's and Guarini's wish for integration expresses a new *psychological* synthesis which unifies traditionally distinct characters.

The possibilities opened up by their works culminated in the works of the great Central European architects of the eighteenth century, Johann Lucas von Hildebrandt, Christoph and Kilian Ignaz Dientzenhofer and Balthasar Neumann. By transforming the massive wall into a system of pillars and filled-in 'membranes', Christoph Dientzenhofer arrived at an adequate 'materialization'

(39) **Francesco Borromini** *S. Ivo* Rome, begun in 1642

31 See P. Portoghesi *Borromini, architettura come linguaggio*, pp. 384ff., also C. Norberg-Schulz 'Borromini e il barocco boemo' Accademia di S. Luca, 1970

32 See C. Norberg-Schulz 'Lo spazio nell'architettura post-guariniana'– Accademia delle Scienze di Torino, 1970

(40) **Guarino Guarini** *S. Filippo* Casale Monferrato 1671: spatial system

(41) **Francesco Borromini** *S. Carlino* Rome: spatial field of façade 1667, after Portoghesi

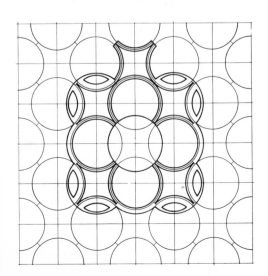

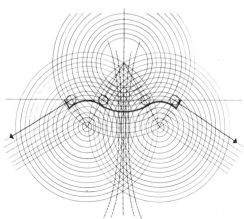

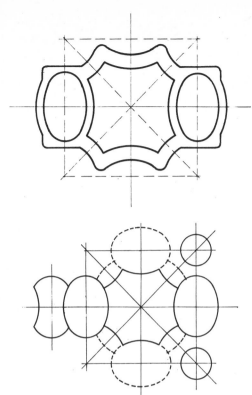

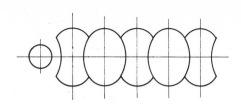

(43) **Kilian Ignaz Dientzenhofer** *combinatory system of spatial elements* early eighteenth century

(44) **Kilian Ignaz Dientzenhofer** *combinatory system of spatial elements* early eighteenth century

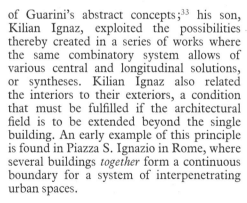

(45) **Filippo Raguzzini** *Piazza di S. Ignazio* Rome 1728

of Guarini's abstract concepts;[33] his son, Kilian Ignaz, exploited the possibilities thereby created in a series of works where the same combinatory system allows of various central and longitudinal solutions, or syntheses. Kilian Ignaz also related the interiors to their exteriors, a condition that must be fulfilled if the architectural field is to be extended beyond the single building. An early example of this principle is found in Piazza S. Ignazio in Rome, where several buildings *together* form a continuous boundary for a system of interpenetrating urban spaces.

Late Baroque architecture thus arrived at integrated architectural fields, where centres, directions and zones work together to form a dynamic totality where any spatial expression is possible. Modern architecture has not gone much further beyond this. The main innovation is a new technology, which makes the extended, 'open' fields implicit in late Baroque architecture materially

33 The solution has its origins in the late-Gothic *Hallenkirche*. See C. Norberg-Schulz *Kilian Ignaz Dientzenhofer e il barocco boemo* 1968

(46) **Theo van Doesburg**
*system of horizontal and
vertical planes c.* 1920

(47) **Paolo Portoghesi**
and **V. Gigliotti** *Casa
Andreis* Scandriglia
1965–1967

34 S. Giedion was the
first to point out late Baroque
space as one of the
'constituent facts' of modern
architecture. See *Space,
time and Architecture* 1941

35 R. Venturi *Complexity
and Contradiction in
Architecture* 1966, p. 72

36 P. Portoghesi and V.
Gigliotti 'Casa Andreis a
Scandriglia, Rieti'
L'architettura 137, March
1967

possible.[34] In the 1920s the ideal was a continuous, flowing space almost completely freed from defined centres and from the distinction between inside and outside. Architects wanted to liberate the static spaces of conventional buildings, to express positively the new 'open' world. Recently, however, the need for defined places and interior spaces has again been felt. As Robert Venturi says: 'The essential purpose of the interiors of buildings is to enclose rather than direct space and to separate the inside from the outside'.[35]

In the Casa Andreis Paolo Portoghesi and Vittorio Gigliotti give a clear demonstration of the actual field concept in architecture, ingeniously exploiting man's previous experiences with architectural space.[36] In accordance with the task set – to build a 'week-end house' – Casa Andreis shows a free and continuous space, with a strong contact between inside and outside. But the space does not float away, neither are qualitative differences wiped out. Casa Andreis collects and divides the surrounding land-

(48) *Casa Andreis*

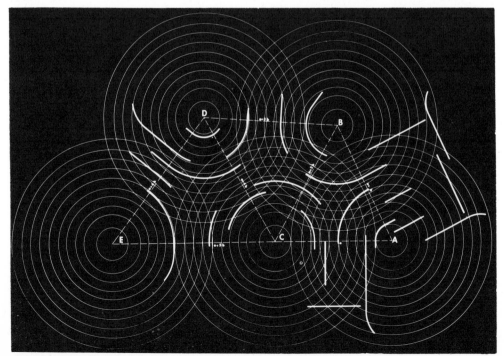

(49) *Casa Andreis*

37 See C. Norberg-Schulz 'Die Architektur von Paolo Portoghesi und Vittorio Gigliotti' Hochschule für Bildende Künste, Hamburg, 1969

scape, bringing the parts together to form a movement which leads up through the tall living-room to the roofscape where it is again united with the environment. This spatial continuity is organized and 'kept' by five foci which define concentric series of circles. Thereby relatively quiet zones are created which capture the surrounding spaces. The circles, however, interfere inside the house, where space becomes like a dynamic stream. The main openings of the house are found in the branches of this stream. Only in the bedrooms is the flow halted by orthogonal walls. Casa Andreis demonstrates how domains may be densified into foci, and how several subordinate foci can interfere to create one complex and richly articulated place, with a particular capacity for rest and movement.[37]

The *genius loci* is thus dependent upon the concrete architectural structure of the environment, which ought to be described in terms of places, paths and domains. Above

(50) *Casa Andreis*

(51) *Casa Andreis*

(52) *Casa Andreis*

(53) *Casa Andreis*

all, *genius loci* means a distinct character. Such a character is never simple, and in our time it is certainly full of complexities and contradictions, but this does not mean that it is without structure or meaning. Any character corresponds to a describable structure, we just have to develop the concepts necessary for its description. Architectural space as a concretization of existential space gives us the key to the problem. Architectural space concretizes man's being in the world.

The levels of architectural space

Hans Sedlmayr was the first to my knowledge to point out that structural analysis has to distinguish between several 'formal levels', which may be governed by *different* principles of organization.[1] We have already discussed the levels of existential space in environmental terms, and therefore do not need to return to the general aspects of the problem. Rather we should ask *how* landscape, city, building and thing are able to concretize the existential levels. The cosmological level can be largely ignored; it cannot be concretized as such, but has to be represented by structures appearing at one of the 'lower' levels. The structure of the geographical level however can, to some

1 H. Sedlmayr 'Zu einer strengen Kunstwissenschaft' *Kunstwissenschaftliche Forschung* I 1931, p. 27

2 See P. Haggett *Locational Analysis in Human Geography* 1965, passim

extent, be transformed by man to fit his environmental image and existential purposes: the Great Chinese Wall is a famous example illustrating man's need for giving a 'better definition' to geography. Obviously the psychic security created by the wall resulted from the widespread *knowledge* of its existence, rather than from individuals perceiving it as part of the landscape level. In the present world we find elements such as military bases which play a similar role. The same holds true for certain national and religious 'monuments' which, although they are architecturally uninteresting, may give structure to a geographic totality. The geographical level is in any case structured by man's economical and practical purposes, and thereby obtains a certain 'meaning'. The planning involved in transforming the geographical level would certainly profit from formulation in terms of places, paths and domains, and, in fact, modern geographical theory has arrived at analogous concepts.[2]

Landscape

The level of landscape concerns the architect more directly. From ancient times we

(55) *Landscape* Sogn, western Norway

(56) *Landscape* southern Norway
(centre above)

can follow man's attempts to make the forms of 'his' landscape more precise, or transform them to fit his general environmental image. The Egyptian pyramids thus constitute an artificial row of mountains defining the boundary of the 'civilized' space along the Nile. Further south in Thebes, where real mountains fulfil the same purpose, pyramids were unnecessary.[3] In general we may say that man, through his works, expresses the capacity of the landscape. As his life takes place in interaction with landscape, this is

3 The temple of Mentuhotep III represents a transitory solution, while Queen Hatshepsut abolished the pyramid altogether. The problem, certainly, also has to be discussed in terms of mortuary symbolism and general architectural development

(57) *Landscape* central Norway

(58) **G. B. Bellucci** (?) *La Rocca* Porto Ercole *c.* 1550

4 In certain zones where a port-population and an inland population live close together, a difference in character which is determined by two different existential spaces, becomes clearly evident. See 'Giglio Castello' *Byggekunst* 6/1969

5 Thus Luther said 'Eine feste Burg ist unser Gott'. See H. Sedlmayr *Die Entstehung der Kathedrale* 1950, p. 120

natural. His settlements, therefore, usually articulate places given by nature, such as the fertile promontory surrounded by unsurmountable mountains, or the protecting harbour on the wind-beaten coast. The 'harbour', in fact, is one of the most generally recognized types of place, and in many languages the word is used as a synonym for security and belonging. Whereas the settlement on a promontory will acquire its identity from clusterlike concentration, as is exemplified in countless Mediterranean villages, the port has the character of enclosure, usually consisting of a continuous row of houses around the water, the real core of this type of place. For people who grow up in a port, the boat, therefore, becomes the meaningful means of movement, offering great freedom in the choice of paths.[4] Through his activities man also articulates the domains implicit in the landscape structure. In farming areas, for instance, we find wonderful patterns of varying domains and sub-domains, with the buildings forming a counterpoint of places. All these examples refer to a naturally 'grown' environment, where physical activities form a constituent force, creating an environmental 'ground' on which man's culture blossoms like a plant. But the landscape level may also be determined from above, that is, by ideologies and beliefs, concretized throughout history by fortifications on the one hand and sanctuaries on the other, structures which express the two basic aspects of man's orientation: physical security and psychic identity. Paradoxically, both share a preference for inaccessible places. The spiritual pilgrimage is made just as difficult as the military conquest. The traditional European landscape was determined by these two elements: the powerful castle and the distant, heavenly sanctuary; sometimes they were unified, as in the famous Mont St Michel, to symbolize the fortified city of Jerusalem.[5] What interests us in this context, is the *transformation of landscape* these ideas achieved. In the Catholic countries, in fact, landscape became *sacred* by the systematic distribution of religious places, from the great sanctuary down to the small crucifix placed along the road. The pilgrimage 'paths' linked these elements to form a meaningful network.

(60) **L. von Hildebrandt**
Belvedere palace Vienna
1720–24

(61) *Harildstad farm* Heidal,
Norway. Houses from the
end of the eighteenth century

6   For the Baroque
landscape see H. Rose
Spätbarock 1922, pp. 16ff

than a geometrical network.[6] The paths of
the park are related to three qualitatively
different domains: the 'civilized' world of the
ornamental *parterre*, the 'tamed' nature of
the *bosquet* (*boschetto*) and the 'wild' nature
of the *selvatico*. These three domains represent three modes of 'dwelling', which are
organized to form a differentiated whole.
The structure becomes complete when we
include the urban milieu found on the other
side of the palace. The palace itself is the
real focus, the home from which man takes
possession of a total, open world. Today
these gardens are usually considered expressions of an absolute passion for power. They
certainly comprise this aspect too, but
behind we find a deep *human* need for a
meaningful relationship to the environment.
The Baroque park, thus, expresses the wish
for humanizing landscape by giving it a
structure corresponding to an integrated, but
varied existential space. Today *everybody*
can enjoy spaces such as Hildebrandt's
Belvedere in Vienna, just as Bach and
Mozart have become accessible to the
general public.

The Renaissance and Baroque periods aimed
at a geometrization of landscape. This first
led to the creation of small formal landscapes, which contrasted with the virgin
nature around. Later, a fusion of formality
and nature was attempted (as in Villa Lante
mentioned above) until the Baroque park
realized a seemingly limitless taking possession of space by means of a system of geometrically organized paths. The structure of
the Baroque landscape, however, is more

Any environmental structure presupposes a
general continuity of landscape space. We
have defined landscape as the 'ground' on

which the structures of the 'lower' levels appear. This basic condition was generally respected in the past: we may look at simple folk architecture, urban settlements or monumental schemes; they always form distinct figures in relation to the landscape. Today, however, a semi-scattered distribution of buildings has become normal and the landscape is broken into fragments, with general visual chaos as a result. Let us therefore stress that buildings either ought to be so scattered that they appear as *individual* figures, or so densely placed that they form *clusters* or *groups*. This principle of 'scattered concentration' seems to be the only possible way of preserving nature as such, rather than reducing it to isolated remains. At the same time we ensure that the settlements become 'things' to which we may have a clear relationship. Yona Friedman has

stretched the idea to its extreme, by suggesting that the populations of Europe be concentrated in a limited number of very large cities forming a network of places and paths.[7] In this way the landscape regains its continuity and its character as background to the works of man. In principle, Friedman's idea means re-establishing the settlement structure which was normal in Europe up to the nineteenth century, but on a different scale in accordance with the needs and the possibilities of our time.

The urban level

It has been maintained that the identity of settlements primarily depends on their figural character in relation to the landscape, and that the scattered concentrations reveal

7 See Y. Friedman *L'architecture mobile* 1970

(62) **Yona Friedman** Europe *c.*1965

(63) *Village* near Luxor, Egypt

(64) *Pitigliano* Tuscany

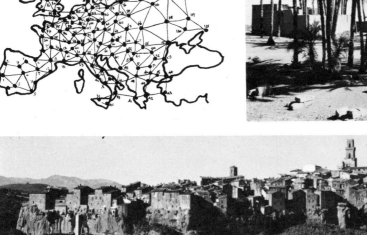

(65) *Village* of the Dogon
tribe, central Africa

(66) *Mölster farm* Voss,
Norway. Houses from the
eighteenth century

(67) Scattering, Cluster,
Ring, Row

a basic environmental structure. But concentrations may be achieved in many different ways – a problem which demands more
attention. It has been shown that any
organization is based on the principles of
proximity, continuity and closure, with the
result that a collection of elements may be
ordered to form a cluster, a row or a ring or
a combination of these structures. We do
not have to turn to psychology to acknow-
ledge these principles. Any farm or village
from any part of the world serves to illustrate
them.[8] In Central Europe, for instance, there
are three basic types of village: the cluster-
village (*Haufendorf*), the lineal village (*Rei-
hendorf*) and the round village (*Rundling*).
The same types are found in Africa, and the
round villages of Sudan and Cameroun and
the clusters of the Dogons have been widely
published. A particularly rich structure is
shown by the Batoufam village in Bamileke,
Cameroun, where several functionally differentiated clusters are interrelated.[9] Splendid
linear villages are found in Indonesia and
Japan. Even in countries where the individual farm acts as a substitute for the
village, analogous types are normal. In
Norway, thus, are found three basic farms:

8   See E. A. Gutkind
*International Encyclopedia
of City Development* vol. I

9   See D. Frazer *Village
Planning in the Primitive
World* 1968

10   See G. Bugge and C.
Norberg-Schulz *Stav og
Laft, Early Wooden
Architecture in Norway* 1969

the cluster-farm on the western coast, the
linear farm in the central valleys, and the
enclosed square farm in the eastern regions.[10]
The three variations on the theme *density*
are obviously determined by different
regional and historical conditions. On the
large open plains or in the extended forests
where nature offers few distinct places, the

enclosed or square forms are usual. In directed valleys the settlements generally have a linear organization: it would anyway be unnatural to create centralized organisms in a space which only offers very particular and limited possibilities of movement. On the Italian hill-tops the cluster is the natural solution, often combined with linear branches of houses along the ridges where paths lead off. All these examples indicate that natural space is never enough to concretize man's existential space. Even the nomads group their tents.

Today these elementary structures seem to have been forgotten. Only quite recently have some architects brought them back to life, often inspired by vernacular architecture. Here we are confronted with a new attitude towards the past: instead of copying

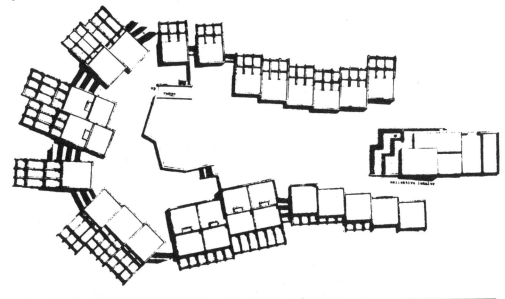

(68) **Jörn Utzon** *Birkehöj*

(69) **Atelier** *5 Siedlung Halen* Berne

its motives, one exploits its general principles. As we have seen, Kevin Lynch has applied analogous principles to the analysis of large cities, but a city is too complex to be defined as a cluster, a row or an enclosure. These basic structures are simply constituent elements of the totality. The *district*, thus may be considered a more or less well defined cluster or group, the *street* is basically a linear formation, and the *square* is an enclosure. The acknowledgement that the basic elements of the city are the district, the street and the square, is in opposition to important trends in contemporary city-planning. The dense district is today generally replaced by a scattered distribution of slab-like buildings, which hardly can be recognized or imagined as a totality, except perhaps from an aeroplane. The modern street has become nothing but a means of communication, lacking architectonic definition, and has accordingly been abolished by a theorist like Hilberseimer. Even if the pedestrian is separated from the cars, the general belief is that he ought to move freely among trees and flowers. And the square, Lynch's 'distinct and unforgettable place', has become a parking lot. As a con-

(70) *Manhattan* aerial view

sequence, many talk about creating 'a new kind of city'. Our analysis of man's existential space, however, shows that the urban level has to be defined in terms of districts, paths and nodes. When this is forgotten, the city ceases to exist, nor can it satisfactorily be replaced by other means of environmental concretization.

Let us therefore take a closer look at the concrete elements of the human city. The main properties of *districts* have already been mentioned in the discussion of the elements of architectural space, and will only need a few supplementary remarks. Topographical circumstances such as a dividing river may, for instance, contribute to the definition of different districts. The seven hills of Rome are another well-known example of topographical differentiation. In any case, it is imperative that some kind of divisions and delimitations be present. If we took the river away from London, Paris or Rome, the formation of a city image would be much more difficult. Even an enormous city like New York presents a natural division in districts. The character of Manhattan is thus determined by its being an island. Its defined circumscription gives us a frame of reference which is basic to the formation of a satisfactory image. Manhattan also shows that districts may become very large without losing their image. It goes without saying that Manhattan itself is divided into several subordinate districts. Greenwich village is a well-known example. Here the crooked streets and the change in scale characterize the zone, and it is significant that it has

(71) *Street* Bologna

become the favourite retreat of artists and intellectuals. In this way New York presents a hierarchical district-structure consisting of superior and subordinate parts. The varying character of city districts gives the townscape the most elementary kind of variation, and guarantees man's possibility of *choice*. So far, the neighbourhood has been considered a mere *functional* unit. The idea of characteristic districts, on the contrary, follows from understanding the basic structure of existential space.

The *street* is a form that is more easily imageable. In the past it was a 'small universe', where the character of the district and of the town as a whole was presented in condensed form to the visitor. The street represented, so to speak, a section of life – history had shaped its details. Today, however, the street is generally lost as a consequence of the current scattering of the buildings and the increasing motorized traffic. But the problem also has other aspects, such as the new immense *scale* which now tends to characterize the streetscape. We are hardly able to identify ourselves with such streets as Park Avenue in New York, and the lack of variation and

(72) *Rothenburg* Bavaria

(73) *Champs Elysées* Paris

spontaneous details is depressing. In general the space-form of the street may be defined as longitudinal, but this does not imply that it ought to be straight. In the towns of the past, oblique angles and curved lines created a 'closed perspective' enlivening the prospect. It is decisive for the spatial character that the buildings appear as *surfaces* rather than masses. If the mass-effect dominates, the *buildings* attain figural character, and by joining the intermediate spaces between them the street is reduced to a subordinate 'ground'. To become a true form, *the street* has to possess 'figural character'. This is achieved by means of a continuous bounding surface, which not only presupposes a certain density, but that the houses belong to the same 'family'. The unification of the street space is furthermore accentuated by the omission of side-walks. The demand that the houses should belong to the same 'family' could obviously result in a dangerous monotony. In the past this was usually counteracted by the houses appearing as variations on the same 'theme'. Such a theme might consist in the repetition of certain proportions, or the emphasizing of properties common to several houses, such as a typical roof, or an arcade on the ground floor. The theme should, however, allow for full freedom in the details. To make the street wall appear as a varied repetition of the same theme, a subdivision into relatively small units is necessary. The large units common today, therefore, do not only destroy human scale, but prevent the street from preserving the varied continuity which is its essence. The principles outlined above were commonly employed up to the nineteenth century, when it became normal to use parallel building lines and uniform heights as ordering means. Historically this change is connected with the concept of the 'parade-street'. The street no longer was intended as an intimate *milieu* for the pedestrian. We have mentioned that the *crossing* has a particular significance in the network of streets, as it represents a choice rather than a goal. It is interesting that towards the end of the fifteenth century, when the city of Ferrara was extended, Biagio Rossetti had already recognized its importance. Thus he stressed the corners of the buildings in order to define the space

83

between them, rather than the buildings themselves.

The *square*, finally, is the most distinct element of the urban structure. As a clearly delimited place it is most easily imageable, and represents a goal for movement. Paul Zucker has characterized it as 'a psychological parking place within the civic landscape'.[11] In the old city atlases two representations generally appear: the city in a bird's-eye view, that is, as a total organism, and the market-place, the core or heart of that organism. Only when reaching the main square had one really *arrived*, and in most old towns the streets lead towards this focal point in a natural way. Even in New York, a metropolis totalling sixteen million inhabitants, Times Square and Washington Square serve as focal points. Even under pronounced 'modern' conditions, thus, the square satisfies basic human needs.

The square is determined by the same formal factors as the street, with the difference that

11 P. Zucker, op. cit., p. 1

(76) *Vigevano*, near Milan, late fifteenth century

the buildings should form a continuity *around* the space. In other words, the effect of different masses has to be reduced in order to obtain a continuous surface. According to their form, many squares appear to be composed of different 'zones'. This facilitates the simultaneous presence of several activities, and also gives the experience a certain variation. Such subdivisions are accentuated by introducing elements such as fountains and monuments, by articulating the pavement, or even by placing a whole building within the space. Because of its size, the square provides the necessary perspective in which to admire main buildings of the town, whose functions as physical and psychological 'landmarks' are thereby accen-

tuated. To remove important public buildings from the core of the urban structure is therefore to destroy it. Generally, the square is marked by a contrast of dimensions, which makes it the climax of the visual experience of the city. The different dimensions should, however, be related to each other in such a way that we may identify ourselves with the whole complex. This is for instance achieved when public buildings appear as particularly outstanding variations of the themes present in the simpler houses.

The elements discussed above and their interrelations, are of topological character. Cities of course are often 'geometrized', but the geometrization is hardly perceived as

85

12 K. Lynch *The Image of the City* 1960, p. 87

such, rather it contributes to the image of certain topological properties (such as domain texture, path continuity or sqaure enclosure). When summing up the general character of environmental images, Kevin Lynch says: 'However distorted, there was a strong element of topological invariance with respect to reality. It was as if the map were drawn on an infinitely flexible rubber sheet; directions were twisted, distances stretched or compressed, large forms so changed from their accurate scale projection as to be at first unrecognizable. But the sequence was usually correct, the map was rarely torn and sewn back together in another order. This continuity is necessary if the image is to be of any value.'[12]

The house

While urban structures have a relatively abstract character, a building is something very concrete and palpable, which is, apparently, more easily imageable. The conscious interest of architects and public, therefore, generally centres on the individual building. To discuss the architectural level of the house thoroughly would mean to present a

theory of architectural form. Such a discussion, however, is not possible within the limits of this book. Let us only say a few words about the 'essence' of the house. To find a common denominator for all houses (buildings) may seem futile. If it makes any

(79) **R. Pietilä** 'a cave of wood' *Dıpoli*, Otaniemi

sense to talk about the 'level of houses', however, it ought to be possible. In fact, all treatises on architecture from Alberti to Venturi in some way or other have attempted to solve the problem. It was pointed out above that essentially the house brings us 'inside'. The essence of the house as architecture, therefore, is *interior space*. In the city we are still 'outside', although we have left the open landscape. In the house we are alone with ourselves, we have withdrawn. When we open our door to others, it is our free decision; we let the world come to us, rather than looking at it outside. 'Domestic peace' has been a basic right since remote times and in a certain sense this also holds true for a public building, which may be considered the home of a well-defined community.

Interior space is primarily thus defined by topological enclosure. But it has also been maintained that any enclosure has to communicate with the environment in varying ways, and that it has a particular interior structure. Thus Venturi says: 'Designing from the outside in, as well as from the inside out, creates necessary tensions, which help make architecture. Since the inside is different from the outside, the wall – the point of change – becomes an architectural event. Architecture occurs at the meeting of interior and exterior forces of use and space. These interior and environmental forces are both general and particular, generic and circumstantial'.[13] Venturi goes on to discuss the problem of the opening at length, and points out the interesting 'double' wall-structures which result when the bounding surface is determined both from within

13 R. Venturi *Complexity and Contradiction in Architecture* 1966, pp. 88f

(80) *Villa Adriana* Tivoli: 'teatro marittimo' *c.* 125

and from without.[14] When we talk about the house as an interior, we do not, therefore, have a structure in mind which necessarily closes itself off from the environment, although the tendency towards isolating the house has been strong throughout architectural history. To be able to withdraw, Hadrian built himself a circular, enclosed house within the Villa Adriana. Significantly, the house is an *island*, surrounded by a moat and an engirdling wall. The Pompeian house, which still represents an unsurpassed solution to the private dwelling, is an enclosed organism. Its contact with the environment is provided for by an axis leading from the entrance to an exedra at the opposite end, but the 'opening' thus created is weak. Rather that creating contact, the axis unifies the interior units of the house, such as the centralized *atrium*, the *tablinum* and the *peristylium*. The Christian church, too, has

(81) *House of the Silver Wedding* Pompei fourth century BC

14 R. Venturi *Complexity and Contradiction in Architecture* 1966, pp. 68ff

(82) *S. Maria della Consolazione* Todi, begun in 1508, architect unknown

always been dominated by enclosure: the centralized organisms of Byzantine and Renaissance architecture, for instance, are enclosed spaces, resting in themselves. In all these cases enclosure has been obtained by centralization or by a continuous, integrated bounding wall. Only the vertical is treated as a symbolic opening. In Borromini's S. Ivo centralization and a continuous engirdling

(84) *La Martorana* Palermo
1148

surface are still present, but the concave-convex movement of the wall indicates that the interior thus defined forms part of a larger context. S. Ivo also shows a completely new *vertical* integration; the space form has been carried without change into the dome. Baroque architecture thus provides a convincing synthesis of the two fundamental aspects of architectural composition: *separation* and *unification*. Articulation, in fact, always consists in the interaction of these two aspects. Spaces, masses and wall elements are separated to express the fact that any building consists of different *parts*, functionally or symbolically determined. As these parts, however, are parts of an *organism*, they must be unified by continuity, repetition (similarity), interdependence or interpenetration.[15]

In orthodox modern architecture the idea of interior space as the essence of the house was

15 For a more extensive discussion of this problem see the chapter on *form* in C. Norberg-Schulz *Intentions in Architecture* 1963, 131ff

(85) **Mies van der Rohe**
National Gallery Berlin
1962–65

(86) **Mies van der Rohe**
National Gallery : interior

(87) **Frank Lloyd Wright**
Herbert F. Johnson residence
'Wingspread' Wind Point,
near Racine, Wisconsin
1937

abolished and replaced by a new ideal of 'flowing space', without distinction between inside and outside. Like most ideals, however, this was scarcely ever put into practice. Even the 'neutral' flowing spaces of Mies van der Rohe are 'anchored', firstly by the strong, regular construction, which often forms a complete centralized whole, and secondly by organizing axes and symmetries. Frank Lloyd Wright, who was the first to attempt a continuous transition between inside and outside,[16] generally organized his directed and 'open' plans around a massive, static core, which was also expressed as a vertical axis. But recently flowing space has been given up as a theoretical ideal altogether. Le Corbusier marked the change in attitude with his wonderful interior at Ronchamp, which communicates with a real and an ideal environment by means of its hovering roof and ingenious openings. Like S. Ivo, the solution expresses a synthetic 'both-and'. In Scharoun's Philharmonic Hall in Berlin the core is a topologically centralized auditorium (a certain axial symmetry, however, is present), expressing the desire to *surround* the content of the building, that is, the performers. This

(88) **Le Corbusier**
Notre Dame du Haut
Ronchamp 1950–53

(89) **H. Scharoun**
Philharmonic Hall Berlin
1956–63

(90) **H. Scharoun**
Philharmonic Hall 1956–63

wonderfully concentrated interior is in turn surrounded by a labyrinthine foyer which, in a fascinating way, expresses the action of coming from outside in and being 'distributed'.

To discuss the variables of interior space in more detail is beyond the scope of this book, but it is worth recalling the primary factors of centralization and continuous boundary, direction, opening and guiding elements, and the secondary properties such as proportion, texture, colour and illumination, which can

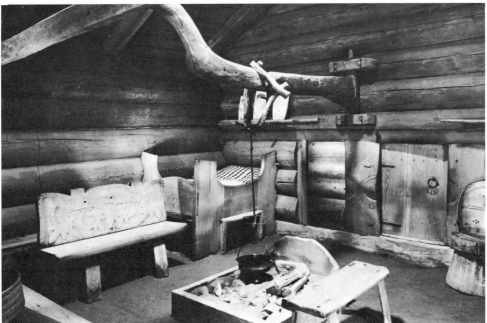

(91) *Norwegian hearth-cottage* Aamli, Setesdal, eighteenth century

be used to reinforce or contradict the primary structure. We should, however, mention the 'things' which particularly help to define the character of the interior. We have already mentioned the fire-place, the bed and the family table as traditional foci of the house. These elements are usually scattered around in the house but in some of the best modern dwellings they are again related to it. The houses of Frank Lloyd Wright in particular offer inspiring illustrations of how to use such elements as functional foci. In a more general way 'things' contribute in giving a house a particular 'atmosphere', varying from the poetic joy of life of the Art Nouveau restaurant to the austere simplicity of the refectory at La Tourette. The existing split

between architect and 'interior decorator' is therefore a meaningless 'differentiation'.

The interaction of levels

The levels of architectural space form a structured totality which corresponds to the structure of existential space. As man's identity is established in relation to the totality of existential space, all the levels of architectural space must have their defined identity. Without it, man's image of his environment will be confused and his own personal identity threatened. The landscape level, thus, is regarded as a ground containing all the particular structures of life and

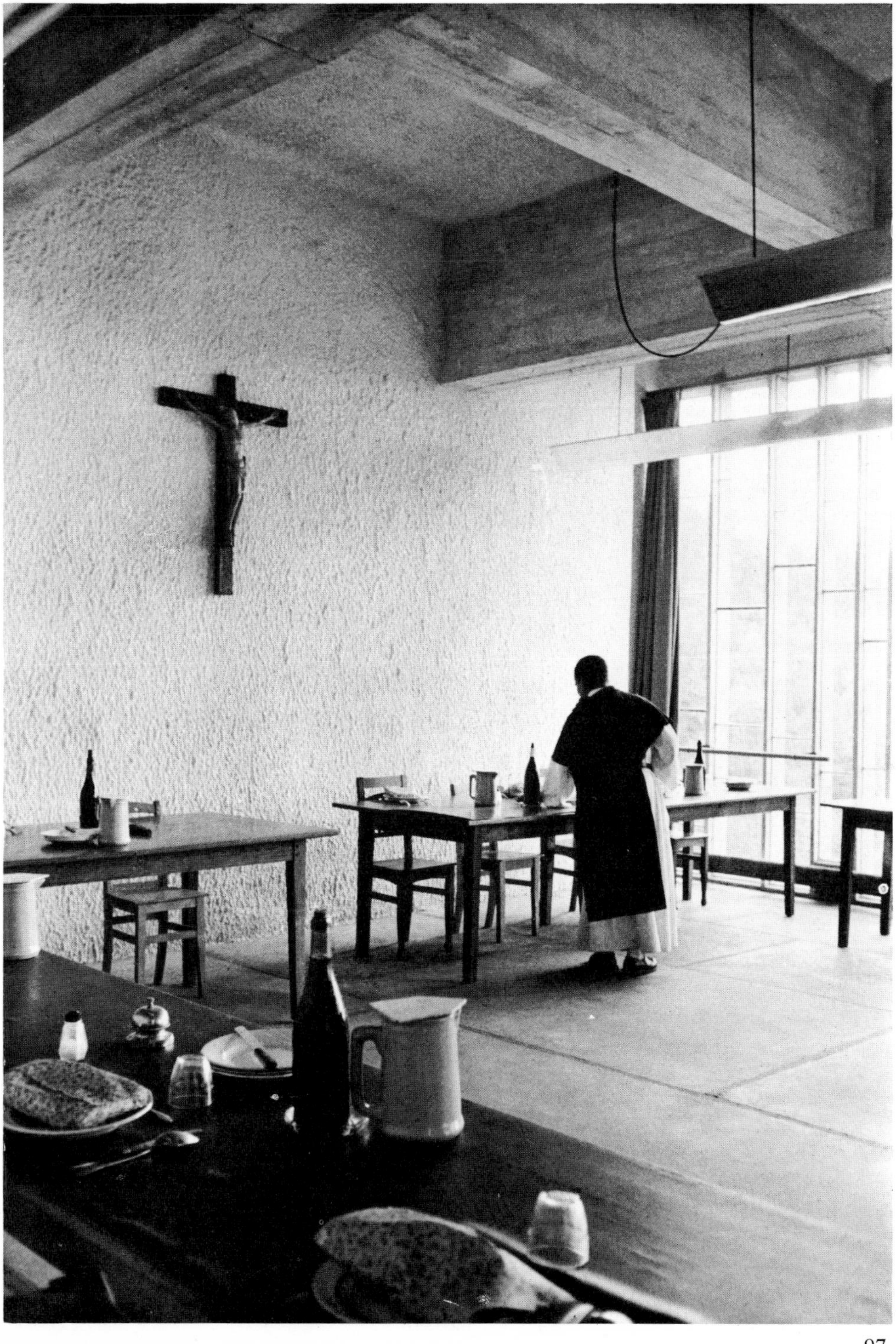

(93) **Le Corbusier**
La Tourette Eveux, near Lyon 1952–60

action: its identity depends upon a general continuity. The urban level is distinguished by concentration and density. Men come together in the city and its identity depends upon this togetherness. The house, however, expresses a certain isolation, a private world which may be closed off at will. In order to satisfy these demands, all the levels ought to have adequate formal properties. Identity means that objects are 'what they want to be', to paraphrase a statement by Louis Kahn.

In general, the levels form a hierarchy. The house, for instance, is essentially interior space but, in relation to the urban level, it functions as a private or public 'landmark' or *Mal*, that is, its properties as a *mass* become relevant. The same holds true for the town itself, which although easily characterized as 'public interior space', in relation to the landscape becomes a concentrated 'form'. Even a whole continent appears as a figure or mass on the geographical level. (A figure, in general, has a higher density than its surroundings.) The twin aspects of space and mass thus recur on every level and we may recall Venturi's statement that 'architecture occurs at the meeting of interior and exterior'. The *wall*, in fact, defines space as

(94) *Delphi* sixth to fourth century BC

well as mass. It is the real concrete element of architecture, although it is determined by more abstract notions of mass and space.

In order to represent each other, the different levels may possess analogous formal characteristics. In principle, representation is achieved by means of 'structural similarity' (isomorphism).[17] Talking about isomorphism the problem of the *archetype* ought to be mentioned. From what has been said above, it is clear that a correspondence between form and content is a necessary property of the world. Form and content are interdependent aspects of the same total experience, with the result that any form has limited possibilities for receiving contents. The archetype, hence, is a reality, but we do not have to introduce a 'collective subconscious' or to study brain processes for its explanation. We should, however, point out that the basic schemata consist of general relationships rather than particular wholes. They enter in ever new combinations and allow for changing interpretations. This tension between basic structure and circumstantial totality signifies that life is both 'constancy and change', to use the words of Giedion.[18]

(95) *Priene* Asia Minor, fourth century BC

The 'field' of existential space is represented (concretized) by a corresponding architectural field. When the fields of the different levels interact, a very complex totality is formed.[19] It may contain different structures on the different levels, and the interaction between them may vary in strength. In classical Greek layouts like Delphi, the landscape level is mainly decided by the meaningful *choice* of a place to settle.[20] The urban level or grouping of the buildings is topologically structured on the basis of enclosure and proximity, whereas the buildings themselves are geometrized and carefully articulated. A Hellenistic town like Priene incorporates a landscape structure in the dual elements of sloping settlement and

17 For the problem of representation and isomorphism see the chapter on *semantics* in C. Norberg-Schulz *Intentions in Architecture* 1963, pp. 167ff

18 S. Giedion 'Constancy, Change and Architecture' *First Gropius Lecture* Harvard University 1961

19 What Venturi has called 'the difficult whole'. *Complexity and Contradiction in Architecture* 1966, p. 89

20 See V. Scully *The Earth, the Temple and the Gods* 1962

(96) *Diocletian's palace* Spalato (Split) (300)

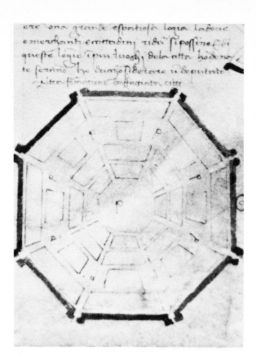

21 This idea was still alive with Alberti, who maintained that private country houses could be rather informal, while the 'perfect forms' (ie circle and regular polygons) ought to be reserved for the church

hill-top Acropolis. The urban level shows a topological circumscription, but orthogonal organization. A variety of structures appear on building level, such as the enclosed private house, topologically organized, the orthogonally articulated agora, and the symmetrical organisms of theatre and temples. A growth in precision from the private over the public to the cultural objects is thereby indicated.[21] A Roman settlement like Diocletian's town palace Spalato (Split) incorporates a fundamental interaction between urban and landscape level by means of the symmetrically disposed arcade facing the sea; the cosmological level is represented by the two crossing streets defining the cardinal points, which divide the town into 'quarters'. The urban level is highly formalized and geometrically integrated but still contains individual, relatively independent buildings such as the temple and the mausoleum. In Renaissance architecture a still more complete interaction of levels was attempted, by basing every building on the same simple geometrical units, and integrating them in a continuous Euclidean space. Here the *same* structure is found on all levels and even nature is given geometrical

(99) **Louis Kahn** *A. N.*
Richards' Laboratories
Philadelphia 1957–61

form in the formal garden. This 'classic' ideal of uniform structure, expressing the image of a harmonious, ordered universe, has continued to haunt architects.[22] It can be found in Mies van der Rohe's modular spaces, which may determine a whole city or even a whole region.[23] The idea seemed convincing as long as it remained on paper or a master like Mies carried out some limited schemes,[24] but its use as a general model has stamped the modern environment with an unbearable monotony. The different levels have lost their individual identity and become a kind of blown up or shrunk versions of each other. As the levels represent different modalities of existence, they ought to be formally different, although they interact and may have some analogous properties. How then can we integrate the fields of the different levels, and concretize the 'difficult whole'? The problem may seem overwhelmingly complex but at its core it is quite simple. Firstly, we have to accept the fact of architectural levels, and realize that each of them need a defined identity. Secondly we should remember that this identity is based on simple topological relationships. A false approach is today concealing these facts, which may consist in either a picturesque play with perceptual effects or in abstract combinatorial geometry. What we need is the true simplicity of the

22 See R. Wittkower *Architectural Principles in the Age of Humanism* 1949

23 See the 'miesian' planning schemes of L. Hilberseimer in *The New City* 1944

24 The same luckily was the fate of the 'ideal city' of the Renaissance

(100) **Louis Kahn** *A. N. Richards' Laboratories* Philadelphia 1957–61

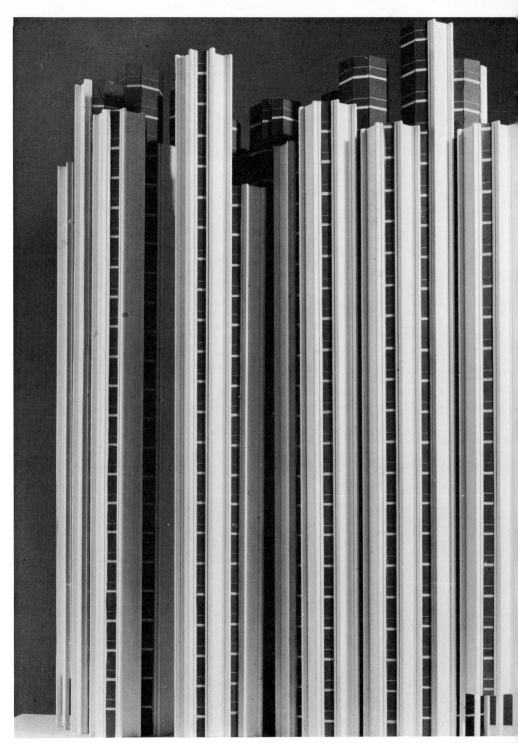

basic structure of existential space, rather than the false simplicity propagated by orthodox modernism. This simplicity, however, when realized in a concrete situation, will often lead to a circumstantially determined complexity. When we analyse a situation in terms of centres, paths and domains, more or less 'open' and more or less complex systems result. Sometimes these systems will be topological in character, but often geometrization is necessary because of the regular repetition of functions or the demands put forward by technological realization. The chief problem, however, is to arrive at a

(102) **Paolo Portoghesi** and **V. Gigliotti** *apartment tower* S. Marinella 1966

25 For a definition of the term 'capacity' see C. Norberg-Schulz *Intentions in Architecture* 1963 pp. 175ff

system with an adequate 'capacity' to satisfy the more or less dynamic aspects of the situation.[25] The capacity of a spatial structure, that is, its ability to receive contents, is determined by its degree of articulation; an inarticulate form can only receive inarticulate contents. If the articulation is 'general', creating a repetition allowing for changes in density, distribution and scale, the space will be capable of covering *several* contents with a certain degree of approximation. If instead, the articulation consists in the establishment of a particular form, the content has to be correspondingly special.

(103) **Paolo Portoghesi** and **V. Gigliotti** *project for the extension of Parliament* Rome 1967

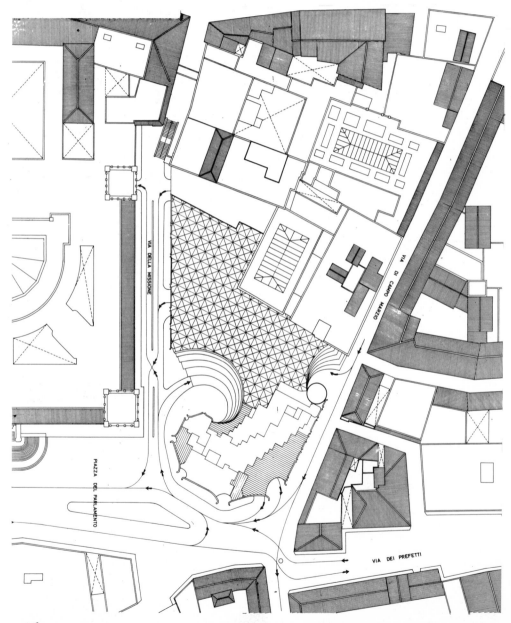

(104–105) **P. Portoghesi** and **V. Gigliotti** *project for the extension of Parliament* Rome 1967

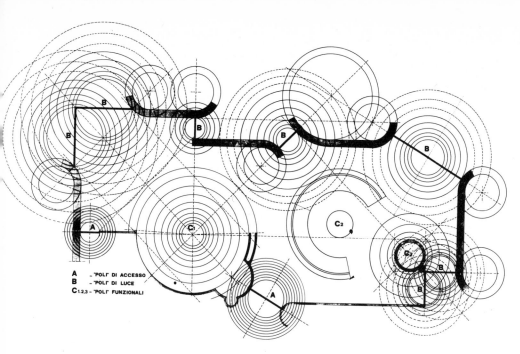

(106) **P. Portoghesi** and **V. Gigliotti** *Casa Papanice* Rome 1969

A - 'POLI' DI ACCESSO
B - 'POLI' DI LUCE
C 1.2.3 - 'POLI' FUNZIONALI

Contemporary architects are greatly preoccupied with these problems. Louis Kahn, for instance, was one of the first to succeed in bringing architecture back to its roots, meanwhile creating more or less open systems with an adequate capacity. Among the members of the younger generation there are those who concentrate their attention on circumstantial complexity, such as Robert Venturi, as well as others who try to develop a more general approach, such as Paolo Portoghesi. It has already been shown that the latter uses geometry to concretize existential space rather than playing with geometrical patterns for their own sake. Projects by Portoghesi and Gigliotti also demonstrate how fields belonging to different levels can be integrated. While the Casa Andreis represented an interaction between the topological structure of the landscape and the geometrically defined system of foci and paths of the house, the project for the extension of the Parliament in Rome illustrates the interaction between a building and the urban level. The complex functions of the building determine a field which has the capacity of receiving a variety of contents. This structure interacts with the environment, not only in the large spiral ramps where 'paths' from outside are let into the building, but mainly in the wall which in its articulation and scale is adapted to the character of Baroque Rome. In many other contemporary projects the building is absorbed by an urban system, without losing its identity. The danger of such a loss of identity seems to be present in the project for the new university in Berlin by Candilis, Josic and Woods. A good illustration is offered by Henning Larsen's scheme for the university in Berlin, where several building structures are integrated by means of a topologically defined urban path. The work of Yona Friedman, finally, differs from that of other 'utopists', as he gives identity to the levels of landscape, settlement and house at the same time as he realizes a general and open infrastructure with a great capacity.

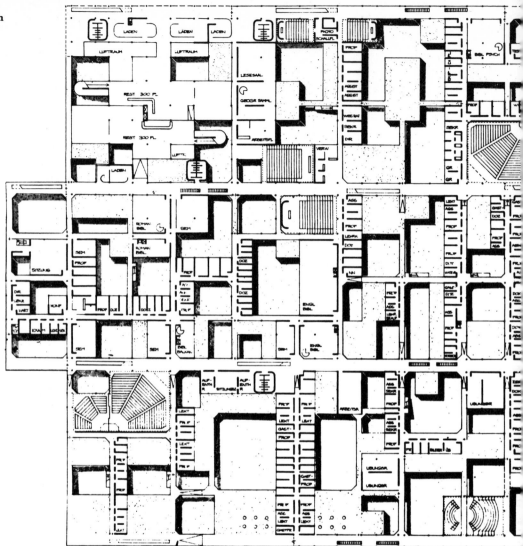

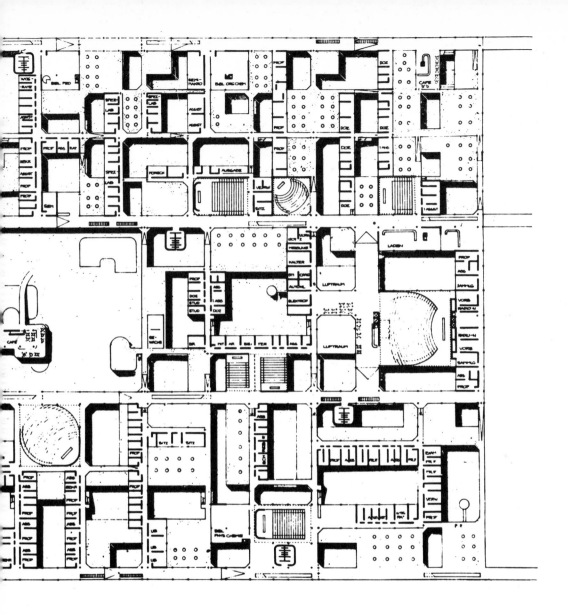

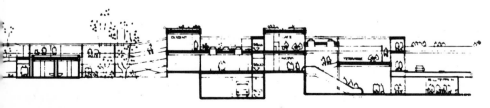

III

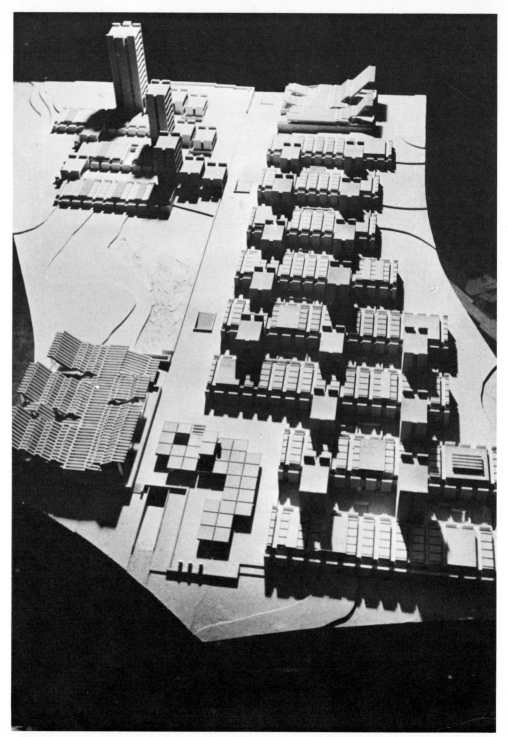

(109) **Yona Friedman**
*project for a city, possibly
Paris* 1965

(110) **Yona Friedman**
*project for a city, possibly
Paris* 1965

Conclusion

I have tried to demonstrate that man's existence is dependent upon the establishment of a meaningful and coherent environmental image or 'existential space'. I have also shown that such an image presupposes the presence of certain concrete environmental (architectural) structures, refusing to accept that these principles lose their significance because of television and rapid means of communication. Architectural space may of course *contain* mobile elements, and its complex structure comprises levels and sub-structures which offer varying degrees of 'freedom'. But it cannot as a totality become mobile. Its general speed of change has to be so slow as to allow for *history*. When history is not related to a stable system of places it becomes meaningless. And, as a matter of fact, a stable system of places offers more freedom than a mobile world. Only in relation to such a system can a 'milieu of possibilities' develop. As Louis Kahn said, 'A city is a place where a small boy, as he walks through it, may see something that will tell him what he wants to do his whole life'.

What, then, must we demand from architectural space in order that man may still call himself *human*? Primarily we must demand an imageable structure that offers rich possibilities for identification. The value of great works of art consists in their allowing for different interpretations without losing their identity. The different 'interpretations' offered by a 'chaotic form', on the contrary, are only arbitrary projections of the self, which burst like soap-bubbles. In ambiguous, complex but structured architectural space we therefore see the alternative to the fatal ideas of mobility and disintegration. This 'unity in plurality' is certainly not a new idea, but it has recently found new interpretations.[26] The task of the architect, therefore, is to help man to find an existential foothold by concretizing his images and dreams.

The concepts of 'home', 'city' and 'country' are still valid. They give a structure to the new 'open' environment and make it possible for us to become citizens of the world. The citizen of the world has *his* place in totality, but by recognizing that it is an element in a larger context, everything else becomes a continuation of his own existential space. The contribution of the individual to totality is to protect and articulate the place he has been given to take care of. This is the meaning of Heidegger's statement: 'Mortals dwell inasmuch as they save the earth . . .'[27] Before he can make a real contribution, man has to *settle*, he has to follow the dictum of Saint-Exupéry: 'I am a builder of cities, I have stopped the caravan on its way. It was only a seed-corn in the wind. But I resist the wind and bury the seed in the earth, to make cedars grow to the honour of God.'[28]

26 It is thus present in Venturi's 'difficult whole', in van Eyck's 'intermediate spaces', in Oskar Hansen's 'open form' and in my own concept of 'intermediary object' (see *Intentions in Architecture* 1963, pp. 179ff)

27 M. Heidegger 'Bauen Wohnen Denken' 1954, p. 24

28 A. de Saint-Exupéry *Citadelle (The Wisdom of the Sands)* 1948

Photo-acknowledgements

The author would like to thank all the architects who so generously supplied illustrations of their own buildings, together with the following for permission to use their photographs in this book: *Aftenposten* 6; Rene Burri-Magnum 13; Widerøe's Flyveselskap A/S 30; A. Winkler, Zurich 69; Freed-Magnum; 70; Alain Perceval 73; Hersteller und Verlag, Lubeck 75; Lucien Hervé 88; Norsk Folke-Museum 91; Cervin Robinson 100; and Oscar Savio 101–106.

Bibliography

Alexander, Christopher *Notes on the Synthesis of Form* Cambridge, Mass 1964
'The City as a Mechanism for Sustaining Human Contact' *Environment of Man* (ed W. R. Ewald) Bloomington 1967

Argan, Giulio Carlo *Progetto e Destino* Rome 1965

Bachelard, Gaston *The Poetics of Space* (trans by M. Jolas) The Orion Press, New York 1964

Bacon, E. N. *Design of Cities* Thames and Hudson, London 1967; Studio Viking, New York 1967

Bandmann, G. *Mittelalterliche Architektur als Bedeutungsträger* Berlin 1951

Bollnow, Otto Friedrich *Mensch und Raum* Stuttgart 1963

Brinckmann, E. A. E. *Bukunst* Tübingen 1956
Deutsche Stadtbaukunst der Vergangenheit Frankfurt 1911
Stadtbaukunst Berlin 1920

Broch, H. *Gedichte* Zürich 1953

Cassirer, Ernst *An Essay on Man* New Haven 1944
The Philosophy of Symbolic Forms (trans by R. Mannheim) (Vol 2) Oxford University Press, London 1955; Yale University Press, 1955

Cook, Peter *Architecture: action and plan* Studio Vista, London 1967; Van Nostrand Reinhold, New York 1967

Critchlow, Keith *Order in Space* London 1969

Dittmar, H. *Der Kampf der Kathedralen* Vienna 1964

Domenig, Gaudenz 'Weg-Ort-Raum' *Bauen + Wohnen* 9/1968

Doxiadis, Constantinos *Ekistics* Hutchinson and Co., London 1968

Einstein, A. *Geometrie und Erfahrung* Berlin 1921

Eliade, Mircea *Patterns in Comparative Religion* (trans by R. Sheed) Sheed and Ward, London 1958; Meridian World Publications n.d.
The Sacred and the Profane (trans by W. R. Trask) Harper and Row, London and New York 1961

Esser, Karl Heinz *Der Architektur-Raum als Erlebnisraum* Bonn 1939

Flavell, John H. *The Developmental Psychology of Jean Piaget* Van Nostrand, Princeton 1963

Frankl, P. *Die Entwicklung der neuen Baukunst* Leipzig 1914

Frazer, D. *Village Planning in the Primitive World* Studio Vista, London and George Braziller, New York 1968

Frey, Dagobert *Gotik und Renaissance als Grundlagen der modernen Weltanschauung* Augsburg 1929
Grundlegung zu einer vergleichenden Kunstwissenschaft Vienna and Innsbruck 1949

Friedman, Y. *L'architecture mobile* Casterman, Tournai 1970

Furth, Hans G. *Piaget and Knowledge* Prentice-Hall, New Jersey 1969

Giedion, Sigfried 'Constancy, Change and Architecture' First Gropius Lecture Harvard University 1961
The Eternal Present II: The Beginnings of Architecture The Clarendon Press, Oxford 1964; Princeton University Press, Princeton 1964
'Die Ungreifbarkeit des Raumes' *Neue Zürcher Zeitung* 22/8-1965

Goldammer, Kurt *Die Formenwelt des Religiösen* Stuttgart 1960

Guidoni, Enrico 'Organicità "in a New Key"' *Marcatre* 16/17/18 (1965)

Gutkind, E. A. *International History of City Development* Vol 1, Free Press 1964

Haan, H. 'Dogon' *Byggekunst* 2/1965

Haggett, Peter *Location Analysis in Human Geography* Edward Arnold, London 1965; St Martin's Press, New York 1965

Hall, E. T. *The Hidden Dimension* New York 1966

Heidegger, Martin 'Bauen Wohnen Denken' *Vorträge und Aufsätze* II Pfullingen 1954
Being and Time (trans by J. Macquarrie and E. Robinson) SCM Press, London 1962; Harper and Row, New York 1962

Hilberseimer, Ludwig *The New City* Chicago 1944

Jammer, Max *Das Problem des Raumes* Darmstadt 1960

Jantzen, H. 'Über den kunstgeschichtlichen Raumbegriff' *Sitzungsberichte der Bayerischen Akademie der Wissenschaften* 1938

Jaspers, K. *Von der Wahrheit* Munich 1947

Jencks, Charles and **Baird, George** (eds) *Meaning in Architecture* Barrie and Jenkins, London 1969

Joedicke, Jürgen 'Vorbemerkung zu einer

Theorie des architektonischen Raumes' *Bauen + Wohnen* 9/1968

Kähler, H. 'Das Fortunaheiligtum von Palestrina Praeneste' *Annales Universitatis Saraviensis* Vol VII, 1958

Kant, I. *Gesammelte Werke* Akademie Ausgabe Vol II

Kästner, E. *Ölberge, Weinberge* Frankfurt 1960

Lee, Terence 'The Psychology of Spatial Orientation' *Architectural Association Quarterly* July 1969

Leonard, Michael 'Humanizing Space' *Progressive Architecture* April 1969

Lévi-Strauss, Claude *Structural Anthropology* Allen Lane, London 1968; Basic Books, New York 1963

Lewin, K. *Principles of Topological Psychology* McGraw Hill, New York 1966
'Der Richtungsbegriff in der Psychologie. Der spezielle und allgemeine hodologische Raum' *Psychologische Forschung* 19 1934

Lynch, Kevin *The Image of the City* M.I.T. Press, Cambridge, Mass. 1960

Maki, Fumihiko *Investigations in Collective Form* St Louis 1964

Merleau-Ponty, Maurice *The Phenomenology of Perception* London 1962; Humanities Press, New York 1962

Minkowski, Eugene *Le temps vécu* Paris 1933

Müller, Werner *Die heilige Stadt* Stuttgart 1961

Netsch, Walter 'Forms as Process' *Progressive Architecture* March 1969

Nitschke, Günter 'Anatomie der gelebten umwelt' *Bauen + Wohnen* 9/1968

Nieuwenhuis, C. 'New Babylon' *Architectural Design* London June 1964

Norberg-Schulz, Christian *Intentions in Architecture* Allen and Unwin, London 1963; M.I.T. Press, Cambridge, Mass. 1968
'Il paesaggio e l'opera dell'uomo' *Edilizia Moderna* 87-88
'Intention und Methode in der Architektur' *Der·Architekt* 6/1967
Kilian Ignaz Dientzenhofer e il barocco boemo Rome 1968
'Sted, rom og eksistens' *Byggekunst* 1968
'Il concetto di luogo' *Controspazio* June 1969
'Borromini e il barocco boemo' Accademia di San Luca 1970

'Lo spazio nell'architettura post-guariniana' Accademia delle Scienze di Torino 1970
'Paolo Portoghesi Vittorio Gigliotti Architektur 1960–1969' Hochschule für bildende Künste Hamburg 1969
'Giglio Castello' *Byggekunst* 6/1969

Parr, Albert Eide 'Problems of Reason, Feeling and Habitat' *Architectural Association Quarterly* July 1969

Parsons, Talcott *Societies* New Jersey 1966; Prentice-Hall, London 1967

Piaget, Jean *The Child's Conception of the World* Routledge and Kegan Paul, London 1929; Humanities Press, New York 1929
The Psychology of Intelligence Routledge and Kegan Paul, London 1950; Littlefield, New York 1968
The Child's Construction of Reality Routledge and Kegan Paul, London 1955; Basic Books, New York 1954
(and **B. Inhelder**) *The Child's Conception of Space* Routledge and Kegan Paul, London 1956; Norton, New York 1967
Le Structuralisme Paris 1968; Basic Books, New York 1970
The Mechanisms of Perception Routledge and Kegan Paul, London 1969; Basic Books, New York 1969
and (**B. Inhelder**) *The Child's Conception of Geometry* Routledge and Kegan Paul, London 1960; Basic Books, New York 1960

Portoghesi, Paolo '*Borromini, architettura come linguaggio* Milan 1967
(and **Gigliotti, V.**) 'Casa Andreis a Scandriglia, Rieti' *L'architettura* 137 March 1967

Rapoport, Amos and **Kantor, Robert E.** 'Complexity and Ambiguity in Environmental Design' *American Institute of Planners Journal* July 1967

Reichenbach, H. *The Rise of Scientific Philosophy* University of California Press 1951

Rose, H. *Spätbarok* Munich 1922

Saint-Exupéry, A. de *The Wisdom of the Sands* (trans by S. Gilbert) Hollis and Carter, London 1952; Harcourt Brace and World n.d.

Schwarz, Rudolf *The Church Incarnate* (trans by C. Harris) Chicago 1958
Von der Bebauung der Erde Heidelberg 1949

Scully, Vincent *The Earth, the Temple and the Gods* Yale University Press, New Haven 1962

Sedlmayr, Hans *Art in Crisis: the lost centre* (trans by B. Battershaw) London 1957
Die Entstehung der Kathedrale Zürich 1950
'Ursprung und Anfänge der Kunst' *Epochen und Werke* I Vienna 1959
'Zu einer strengen Kunstwissenschaft' *Kunstwissenschaftliche Forschungen* I Berlin 1931

Sommer, R. *Personal Space* Prentice-Hall, London and New Jersey 1969

Spengler, Oswald *The Decline of the West* (trans by C. F. Atkinson) Allen and Unwin Ltd, London 1934; Alfred A. Knopf, New York 1945 (2 vols)

Vogt-Göknil, U. *Architektonische Grundbegriffe und Umraumerlebnis* Zürich 1951

von Dürckheim, Graf K. 'Untersuchung zum gelebten Raum' *Neue Psychologishe Studien* 6 Munich 1932

von Uexküll, Jakob *Streifzüge durch die Umwelten von Tieren und Menschen* Hamburg 1956

Venturi, Robert *Complexity and Contradiction in Architecture* Museum of Modern Art, New York 1967

Webber, Melvin M. (ed) *Explorations into Urban Structure* University of Pennsylvania Press, Philadelphia 1963

Weiss, Richard *Häuser und Landschaften der Schweiz* Zürich 1959

Werner, H. *Comparative Psychology of Mental Development* New York 1957 (2nd printing)

Wertheimer 'Laws of Organization in Perceptual Forms' *A Source Book of Gestalt Psychology* (ed W. D. Ellis) London 1938

Wittkower, R. *Architectural Principles in the Age of Humanism* Tiranti Ltd, London 1949; revised ed. 1962; Random House, New York 1965

Zevi, Bruno *Architecture and Space* (trans by M. Gendel) Horizon Press, New York 1957

Zucker, Paul *Town and Square* Oxford University Press, London 1959; Columbia University Press, New York 1959

Index, persons

Index